Selling Emotionally Transformative Services

Business and Self-Worth Advice
Holistic Practitioners
Need to Know

By Todd Schaefer

All rights to this book belong to Todd Schaefer

As You Wish Publishing, LLC

Kyra@asyouwishpublishing.com 602-592-1141

ISBN-13: 978-1-7324982-5-9

ISBN-10: 1-7324982-5-3

Library of Congress Control Number: 2019903277

Edited by Rhonda Carroll

Printed in the United States of America.

Table Of Contents

Foreword by Kyra Schaefer

This book is small, but mighty. It will teach you how to increase your sales, get organized, and build your self-worth to help you give more to the world.

The biggest challenge I have noticed with holistic, alternative and healer practitioners is that they often quit their practice after a year, before they've given their business a chance to succeed. They start with passion and a talent for offering services, but then discover that they can't sell their services. They were never taught how to be a business person in an alternative industry.

Most instructors who teach the classes, modalities and certifications that holistic practitioners pursue have never had successful practices themselves, making it difficult for them to preach business success to their students. They sell a new healer on the dream of having tons of clients without giving them all the skills necessary to achieve their goals. Because they are not taught how to *run* their businesses, holistic practitioners will feel discouraged and lose interest, especially if they have self-worth issues in asking for money for their services. This book changes all of that.

When Todd first taught me this sales system, I was resistant and reluctant to put every aspect of it into action. My reluctance came from several old beliefs I carried with me such as: "This is God given, I should only charge what they can pay," "I'm not an expert, why should they pay me?" "People resist me when I ask them to pay," "I don't feel comfortable asking for money," "I can't guarantee they will be healed, what are they paying me for?" And on and on. I would consistently talk myself (and my clients) out of buying my services.

Once I put Todd's system in place, I could see that clients *wanted* to pay an equal exchange for my services. They *wanted* to keep working with me and they needed what I had to offer. I noticed that their willingness to take responsibility for themselves increased and they completed the homework I assigned. My clients would make larger leaps in their personal development because they *owned* their transformation and they no longer relied on me to do it for them. Using this system helped me sell to so many clients that I referred clients to other practitioners when my scheduling book became too full. I even hired staff to help me with daily operations due to my client volume. My success with sales provided me the opportunity to share my abundance by employing staff.

It is important that you decide what is best for you. It may take time and practice (as it did for me), but if you follow this system line by line—you *will* sell. In the first year of running my business alone (with my limiting beliefs intact), I made $9,000. In my second year of business, Todd examined the business issues I faced and helped me correct my lingering self-doubt. I followed the system you are about to learn, and we made $50,000 that second year. I was working less and I had fewer tears. In the following years, we helped thousands of people and made hundreds of thousands of dollars.

If your heart is meant to perform alternative and holistic work and you have a passion for helping people, please don't give up. Money loves structure. Find that structure and you will help thousands of people and they, in turn, will help thousands more. If that means giving up a little fear and trusting that this information has found you for a *reason*, follow your intuition and discover what happens. You deserve abundance and your clients need you to show them that they can value your work and own their healing journey with your unique guidance and love.

Preface

This book will help you increase your self-worth so that you can step into your power and authentically sell to clients. It will guide your approach so that you feel like you're connecting instead of selling. It will encourage you, so that by the time you're finished speaking with your potential client, they will feel cared for, and they will *want* to buy from you—before you even offer the sale.

People want to be profitable and successful, and then they discover they don't have the self-worth to be that way. That's like having a big ship with a little rudder. In this book, we're going to make your ship's rudder bigger so that you can shift course and start heading to Pleasure Island and Profit Town.

As non-traditional business owners, we're willing to make that special effort for our clients, but we don't always have the same attitude for ourselves. Why not? If we don't have a firm sense of self-worth, we will experience roadblocks and obstacles as we go into business. We can say that we want to be successful, and we do our best to progress toward success, but we may not yet have the worthiness to allow success.

Have you ever asked yourself, "If I try to become more successful with my business, am I going to be seen as a fraud?" Or, "Am I worthy to receive this person's hard-earned money?"

I created this book from what I've learned about self-worth in business, and I've designed a sales system that caters to the sensitivities of non-traditional business owners. I will strengthen your self-worth while teaching you sustainable, authentic selling skills. As a fellow healer, I know where your pain points are and where you're likely to struggle, so I've set up safety nets beneath the tight rope of business ownership. I'll give you a self-worth overhaul while providing a structured template for doing the tasks that may not come easily for you. I'll maximize your strengths and minimize your weaknesses.

You became a healer because you have talents to share and because you naturally feel your way through your thought processes and decision-making methods. You know how to sense inconsistencies with other people (and yourself). You want to use your strengths to your advantage. Although commonplace in most businesses, "powering through things" without an intuitive approach doesn't feel authentic to you. You have so many brilliant faculties, yet your business doesn't reflect that. Let's change that.

As I walk with you through this book, you will notice your prism of light becoming clearer. It's so much easier to shine when you know what to say, how to read your client and avoid unnecessary pitfalls. Authentic selling is approaching your business in a way that's helping you and the client while making sure you're not sabotaging yourself or the client.

This book doesn't contain all of the answers. Don't worry about making mistakes because mistakes are natural, and bumping into walls is how you learn. If you're allowing yourself to make mistakes, you're ahead of the game because that's better than someone who doesn't let themselves try for fear of making mistakes. The difference now is that by reading this book, you will drastically reduce your learning curve and will overcome personal blocks that would have otherwise held you back for years to come.

This book has helped me and others step into their power. Hopefully, as you read, you'll gain many insights and awareness which will help you toward becoming a worthy, authentic, successful business owner.

Introduction

Many non-traditional serviced-based business owner practitioners are not bound by the same regulations, restraints and conditions as traditional business owners. These business owners are largely alternative and holistic and, generally, arrive in the market with no professional business background or knowledge-base for creating and managing their practice. Virtually all have talented skill sets and, perhaps, numerous certifications. As spirited pioneers in the largely standardized world of business, these practitioners brave the storms of getting organized enough to make an impact.

While many of these meek folk tend to incubate and stay under the radar, many are beginning to strike out in bigger ways, going "all-in" and taking bigger risks to succeed in business and make an impact with their services. They've felt the call to step out. They're following their intuition. They're filling the void of emotional emptiness that the populous is screaming out for. These "healers" are needed.

This book is for the non-traditional business practitioner.

It's for the holistic, alternative, healer-type person-alities who have a talent for offering transformational business services, but who need to get organized in their businesses. This book will help you improve your self-worth and get organized, particularly with selling your services to clients.

I'll be referring to my target audience throughout this book, which includes the following: *non-traditional, holistic, alternative, healer, service-based business owners who are practitioners and see clients 1-on-1 performing emotionally transformative services and who want to sell packages of sessions to their clients.* But instead of writing all of that out each time, I will refer to this entire group as "Non-Traditional Business Owners" or "NBOs." Also, since this book primarily deals with sales, whenever you see me refer to the "client," you may assume that I mean the "potential client" whom you are qualifying for a sale.

If you are familiar with the Myers-Briggs Type Indicator (MBTI), "Intuitive Feelers" (NFs) or "Feelers" (Fs) will benefit the most from this book. Most healers will be NFs. You can test to discover your type online for free at various websites. To ensure the best test accuracy, I recommend you choose a binary test which provides only two responses per question. Tests that allow you to rank yourself within a range of disagree/neutral/agree options for each question will not provide accurate test results. The test results will show your type (i.e., INFJ) and provide a helpful explanation to show how your personality type thinks and makes decisions which will further support you in your business.

While part-time NBOs can greatly benefit from the principles and content herein, the book is primarily designed for business owners who intend to be full-time practitioners. I need to say this because part-timers may not be motivated to experience greater business success, and will likely not be incentivized to implement everything I teach. For them, this book may be overkill. But, if you are a part-timer and are motivated to "go bigger," or you have already invested significant expense into your business or making your business your full-time endeavor, then this book is for you. When you've invested your time and real dollars into your business, you're serious and determined to succeed. This book is for all NBOs who are committed because they have already invested in themselves and their businesses.

In coaching many NBOs, I've learned that their biggest challenges are one or more of the following: 1) they want to expand, but they have personal blocks to allowing greater abundance, or 2) they have talent, but they don't understand how to run their business to the level of success they would prefer to achieve. This book will help you remove those blocks and take you through a *systematized, predictable sales process* so that you will feel good in your sales approach and your clients will love you as a result.

This book will help NBOs like you to provide better service for your clients by implementing a *free 30-minute Intake Assessment.* When you correctly conduct your Intake Assessment, it will help you make more money by selling packages of sessions, discover and retain all-star clients who give stellar online reviews and referrals, and protect your business from less than ideal ("dud") clients who could result in negative online reviews. While the book can be used for other sales applications, it is primarily designed for use in a 1-on-1 environment with a client.

If your business is truly a one-stop shop (or novelty business) and you have no need of working with clients long-term to provide deeper, lasting results for them, then this book will be excessive. Nevertheless, I urge you to consider using this sales system, perform it correctly, and create package sales to do your best work to help your clients transform. No matter what type of business you have, ask yourself, *"Could I achieve better results for my clients if they saw me for a series of sessions instead of one session?"*

This book will leverage your best strengths, natural humility and authenticity in a way that feels completely seamless and effortless and feels good to your clients. While you read, I'll help you avoid pitfalls. I'll emphasize things that are important. I'll give you a comprehensive understanding of what to do and how to do it. I'll show you what to look for and how to know when it's appropriate to sell and when not to sell. I'll make asking for the sale *easy*.

I strongly recommend that you read the book in sequential order and do not skip any sections. It's crucial that you thoroughly understand the entire sales process so that there are no gaps in your understanding.

I have no business background. However, I have made over $300,000 in three years in my business by implementing what I will teach you in this book, and many of my clients have chosen me to coach them for years after

I've helped them with their initial reasons for working with me. Nevertheless, money was never my ultimate motive and it may not be yours either. It's possible that you might not even want to make a lot of money. You might want to define success on your terms. Your driver is likely being authentic while you become profitable. After all, who would want to be successful if he or she felt insincere while making sales and people hated them as a result?

You may need to read this book a few times to retain all of its content, and I recommend you do. Understanding and practicing the content will make you a better salesperson—*not* using fancy sales questions. I've watched NBOs skip the sales training in the past and go immediately to using the sales questions I gave them. They got excited about their "magical success," and then became disillusioned when the magic no longer worked. Can you guess why? *They didn't learn anything.*

Learning sales and getting organized is a long-term investment. What you learn in this book will apply to anything you want to sell in the future. By the way, do you plan to see clients 1-on-1 until you retire? Or will you eventually want to do something bigger? Like, write a book? Or host retreats and telesummits? Or speak in front of audiences that pay you to share your knowledge with them? No matter how your business evolves, you take your sales skills with you.

Different businesses may have various restrictions on how they can and can't run their businesses or have regulations they must adhere to, but this book isn't about jumping through any regulatory hoops in any specific industry. Instead, I will show you how my sales system worked for my alternative industry (life coaching and hypnotherapy) and how it continues to work for the many business owners I've taught. In time, you will emulate our success on your terms. Thus, if you want to upgrade your sales skills, your profits and your client relationships in a completely authentic manner that feels great to you, then look no further than this book. Take your time and enjoy it. I will walk you through every single step.

Remember, it doesn't matter what you are selling; it matters that your clients trust you and connect with you. If they trust you and you are authentic and trustworthy, then the client will believe that you can help them. The rest is up to you.

Chapter 1 - Cleansing the Palette

Before we get into the bulk of the book, we need to address some spiritual falsehoods which many NBO's need to reconcile before they can become successful and profitable. The goal in this opening chapter is to help you to resolve these false beliefs so that you give yourself permission to take your next steps in business.

This is the only chapter where I will mention "God." Whatever I say about God that you feel doesn't apply to you, feel free to throw it out. You can substitute whatever you want in its place: spirit, Holy Spirit, higher self, source, or universe. The goal here is to *resolve* any misconceptions you might have about being worthy and receiving money. For your reference, the principles that I speak of about God and worthiness are rooted in *A Course in Miracles* (ACIM).

Only Your Willingness is Needed

The only thing you need to be "open to receiving" and "being worthy" is your willingness to be *shown* that you're worthy. That means allowing God and the Holy Spirit to remove what is false in you to reveal your inherent worthiness. The reason it's so hard to establish your worthiness is because you didn't create your worthiness— God did. That means you will realize your worthiness by allowing yourself to remember that God has established your worth.

It's Natural for You to Be Abundant

If you can agree that God established your worth (and not you), why would God not want you to receive the fruits from your talents which God created in you?

Money comes when you feel good. Abundance arrives when you feel the least resistant. You should be receiving money for your God-Given talents *because* it is God's will for you to receive money.

Charging for Your God-Given Talents

You might be thinking, "My talents are given to me by God. Why should I charge for them? Everyone should have what I want to give!"

As an NBO, you're not charging for your God-given ability. You're charging for your time, your skill level, your years of dedication to your craft, your perseverance throughout your failures, lean times and exhaustion. You're charging for your willingness to learn and to keep putting one foot in front of the other. You're charging for never giving up while facing the impossible. Do you want to be able to provide for all your needs so that you can see more clients? Then you need to charge for your time and your personal investments.

When you say, "This is God-given, and you need my service," you make yourself 'special,' according to ACIM, and the need for specialness means you're in business to prove that you're worthy. At that point, it's no longer about serving the client; it's about serving yourself.

Saying that your service should be free means, you're not taking responsibility for your talent, and you don't want to be held accountable to those you help or the service you provide. When no one has anything to expect from you, you can freely serve them without fearing judgment by others while not having to face your fears of failure and success.

If you insist on not receiving any money, then your bills aren't getting paid and you're not able to see more clients. Your choice not to receive money would prevent you from using your God-given talent. There's nothing spiritual about not allowing abundance. It is completely unspiritual to be broke and to be making "just enough." It is spiritual to have money—lots of it! The universe is set up to support you.

The household names in the spiritual industry who speak at conferences and write books that you talk about with your friends—are they able to receive? What would these big names say about money? Would they say that you should charge appropriately for your services? Would they say that you need to build solid self-worth to be successful? Yes, they would, because *people who can't receive can't be examples to other people.*

When You're Worthy, You're Receiving

Being able to receive means *you're not guilty.* You're allowed to *receive* the love of God. You don't have to make yourself worthy to receive God's love. You don't work harder to be worthy; you *allow* to be worthy. You relax to be worthy. If you feel that you have to work at something to be worthy, then you are usurping God's will—that's "arrogance," according to ACIM. When the mind is quiet and not fighting, inspiration occurs because you're in the most *receptive* mode. Going against the grain looks like trying hard to prove you're worthy of receiving, and that's a cyclical ego trap. Receiving is of God.

When you feel good from offering your service, do you notice how you naturally receive and attract more good things? Do you notice how clients *want* to pay you in gratitude for the great service you provided for them? When clients receive value from you, they *want* to give back. Abundance shows up most when you feel good and believe good things about yourself. If you're believing poor things about your worthiness and that receiving money is not Godly, then you'll attract people who believe that spiritual work should be cheap or free.

Allowing What is False in You to Be Removed

Your self-doubt, unworthiness, false humility, fear of what others think of you and more is the ego—your false self. It's not you.

From *A Course in Miracles* perspective, you reach God's kingdom by allowing everything that is false in you to be removed. All of the love and desire to be of service is the love in you. If you think about your self-worth in these terms, it becomes clear rather quickly that all you need to do is recognize what's driving your self-worth at any given moment—love or fear? God or ego? There is no more need to fight over, run from, or justify and defend what you think you don't deserve.

Ego's version of your success might look like you staying in poverty or you becoming successful, having money, and taking all of your limiting beliefs with you. But ego cannot come with you into God's definition of success for you. The more successful you become, the more you will be required to transcend your limiting beliefs of the ego. You will be called into higher levels of service to the extent that you can release those false beliefs. If you're stuck in unworthiness and uncomfortable that your business has been stagnant, and you're looking for ways to climb higher, these are the things to start unraveling.

The ego wants you to fight with yourself. It wants you to get stuck in its web of lies. When you allow this, you've lost the game. Don't settle for fighting with your ego. Don't settle for less than what God wants you to have, which is everything. God loves us and reminds us that there is no need for sacrifice or fear, and that we are responsible for removing them. This book is designed to assist NBOs like you who are ready to move beyond old limitations, who want to embrace more of their worthiness, get out of fear and into love and receiving.

Anything that makes you believe that the "better you feel, the less you should charge" is a complete lie. It's a web spun by the ego. Your ego is trying to say, "Hey, you have to prove yourself. You can't be worthy and receive."

When you feel that lie show up, it's time to completely reevaluate and say, "Whoa stop! Cancel that! Cancel, clear! I see that my ego is trying to impose guilt upon me, and it's being seductive about it. Cancel that thought!" If your business isn't growing the way you want it to, it's because ego falsehoods are in place trying to fulfill *themselves* in your business, using you as their host.

Chapter 1 Summary

- Addressing spiritual falsehoods
- What you need, to be worthy
- Do you charge for your talent or your time?
- How to remove ego's lies about yourself

Chapter 2 - Self-Worth

Why Your Business Isn't Growing

Besides having a lack of self-worth, NBO's who say they want business growth but don't allow growth do so for one primary reason: they are getting something out of staying where they are and, therefore, aren't incentivized to grow. If you say you want business growth, but you're not allowing it, you need to ask yourself, "What am I getting out of staying where I am?" I promise you; there is a reason. It could be safety, fear of what others' think of you or any number of perceived false realities.

Your ego mind (10 percent of you) is the part of you that thinks you need to "go bigger." But your emotional mind (or subconscious mind; 90 percent of you) is the part of you that makes up the majority of your programming and determines why you feel the way you do about everything. So, your ego mind may want to "go bigger," but the majority of you that lives in your feelings may not be ready to go bigger, or may feel a certain amount of safety in staying where you are and doing what you've always done. This holds for all beliefs you have: money, worth and jobs.

You are Worthy to Receive

Ask yourself what example you want to set for your family, friends, children, grandchildren about their worth. After you die, will they say the following about you?

"Yeah, my mom (or dad, grandma, grandpa) was a great healer, but she (or he) charged too little for her services. She was an amazing person, but she didn't believe she was worthy. So yeah, when I grew up, I figured working for minimum wage was the life for me. No need to go into business for myself or be anything more. She *did* teach me to have integrity, to do what I love, to marry whomever I want, and to live life with joy, but when it came to money and being worthy to receive, well, I don't know much about that. I don't blame her for not feeling worthy of having money. She never taught me "bad" things about money. It was never talked about, and I think that somehow translated to what I feel I deserve to have for myself—so I settled."

Does any of that make you angry or sad? Your worthiness or unworthiness is setting an example for your loved ones. Now, think about this: Is it *still* worthwhile not to receive more? Don't defend your limitations. There's a difference between being charitable and defending a position. I know you've had a challenging past. I honor that. I'm not here to make you feel wrong about what you've been through. I am here to ask you: no matter how good or bad your past has been, how long do you want to carry around that old story? Is it still serving you? What do you want your story to be?

In the not so far-off future, NBOs who are *not* able to receive money and be worthy are going to be dismissed and left behind, unless they choose to step up. They will be left behind in the wake of the mass movement of people who are allowing themselves to accept their birthright of worthiness. If you are resisting me as you read this and fighting for your limitation saying, "I just want to help everyone!" I would challenge your lack of self-worth, no matter your resistance to it. Anyone who fights for their limitation does so, only because they want to keep it. Anyone who proclaims their worthiness and receives is in love.

Practice Blowing Your Horn

Have you ever heard the quote, "If you don't blow your own horn, someone else will use it as a spittoon"? Many authentic business owners would rather not be successful than be seen as "unspiritual" or "not humble." However people are so focused on being humble that they forget to be worthy. The humility I speak of is false humility. The fear of being seen as not humble is about approval, not humility. So purge humility from your mind. Being truly humble is about not letting your fearful ego guide your decisions, but checking in with your inner source for each choice and letting it guide you. Mastery is distinguishing between the two. Being humble is allowing energy to serve you. It's about allowing abundance. Step through any feelings of low self-worth and practice projecting confidence. That's all it takes. Do it repetitively. Read this section as many times as you need to. Nothing—*nothing*—makes you unworthy of receiving everything. You are worthy. Anything less than your complete, unwavering worthiness is only a temporary lie that you've bought into, easily released by your decision to let it go.

You have to practice teaching, practice selling, practice allowing, practice being worthy. Who told you to settle? Who convinced you to buy into that lie? Put some spit on your tuba and blow your own horn. Allow yourself to feel good about your accomplishments. Allow yourself to step out of your comfort zone for the things you believe in. "Inch by inch is a cinch." You can overcome and breakthrough anything if you know why you're doing it and you break it down into a series of steps. If you don't, you'll know it because you'll slip back into your shell of self-sabotage and self-protection. Then no one wins. Not you, not the client whom you could have helped. Practicing keeps you on your game and your wheels greased.

Check your Ego at the Door

Concentrate and fully commit to your clients' success. Stop trying to get what you want and focus on helping them get what they want. If you're in business to prove your worth, be validated, get approval or people-please, you won't get far. If you're in business to heal yourself, you won't get far. Don't use clients to create your safety. Don't try to "get" from them. If you have any of these things going on, then you have an authenticity problem because you think you're there to be of service, but you're there to get approval from your clients.

Fear of Losing Approval

What underlies the fear of selling? It is the fear of losing approval from others. This is the biggest fear that people have, especially NBOs. This fear is a big reason why NBOs like you need a sales system you can rely on so that your lack of self-worth is not dictating your actions when working with clients.

The fear of losing approval from others is the biggest reason we self-sabotage, don't attract clients and don't sell. Approval-seeking comes from our childhood conditioning. If you're burdened with people-pleasing and approval-seeking behaviors occurring in your relationships with family and friends, then you will relate to your clients the same way. You don't want the fear of not being liked by people sabotaging your ability to sell to them or be successful. Would you want your self-generated fears sabotaging your success? You're in business to bring service to your clients, care about them and get paid handsomely for it.

People-pleasing and approval seeking behaviors might include beliefs about your worthiness to receive money, feeling worthless as a person and fear of the client thinking of you as a fraud. You don't have to worry about people feeling like you're a fraud. You are completely worthy and lovable as you are, and you owe it to yourself to keep taking steps, whether they are small steps or big steps.

You're completely authentic, lovable and worthy, and you have to believe in yourself even when you're afraid because you know that's what it's going to take.

What is Failure?

Failure is deciding for yourself ahead of time that the client wouldn't want your service, so you decide not even to bother offering your service or offering a substandard version of it. You talk yourself out of asking for the sale. That's failure—self-sabotage and self-defeat. Notice that I did *not* say that failure is trying your best to sell and then making no sales. That's not failure; that's a learning curve. True failure is convincing yourself not to try. You might think that failing is quitting, but it's not. Quitting is stopping when you want to stop. Failing is quitting when your heart's still in it.

If you read about the most successful business owners in the world, you'll find that they've failed as much as they've succeeded. They've lost millions but then gained it all back and more in a matter of months because they chose to learn from their mistakes and upgraded their mindsets. When you choose to upgrade your mindset, your abundance is a non-issue.

When you upgrade your self-worth, you can gain money, lose money and gain it back again. Failures become learning experiences to catapult your growth and make wise future decisions instead of allowing something that happened to define you permanently.

Self-Sabotage

Remember this quote:

"Whatever level of success we allow for ourselves is a direct reflection of our beliefs about what we feel we deserve."

That quote is the sublime definition of self-sabotage. If you don't feel like you deserve it, then it doesn't matter how much you say you want to be successful. If you feel like you don't deserve it, you unconsciously won't attract it. You must practice being worthy if you want to make money. It's time to take the focus from others' opinions, and focus on serving your client. Put blinders on how you see others reacting to you.

If you're experiencing a block in your business, you need to ask yourself the following questions:

What am I afraid of right now? What am I resisting right now? What lie am I believing about myself right now?

Ask yourself these questions any time you go into fear. Asking will create distance between yourself and the fearful, antiquated ego that is trying to protect you. The fear is what's telling you that you're not good enough. If you think you're unworthy, the ego is winning its game against you. You do not have to put up with that. You are good enough. If you react to your fears, you will make poor decisions such as discounting prices, giving free sessions, abandoning the sale, making impulse or premature business-related purchases, backtracking and creating unnecessary busyness.

When you ask yourself the above questions anytime you're in fear, your subconscious mind is eventually going to answer your question, and you're going to get an "A-ha!" moment at some point. This moment could arrive in a matter of seconds or days, or could come to you in a dream or as a sudden inspiration. I suggest asking yourself these questions at bedtime to allow your subconscious to work on the issue while you sleep. When you receive your "A-ha!" moment, write your insight down and explore your new awareness about it. Then post it somewhere where you can refer to it. Read your new affirmation, or positive insights frequently to weed out future doubtful thoughts as they arrive. Then, congratulate yourself for actively upgrading your mindset and your self-worth.

Chapter 2 Summary

- Why your business isn't growing
- How to promote yourself
- The fear of losing client approval
- Quitting vs. failing
- Self-sabotage

Chapter 3 - Clients

If a client is inspired to take personal responsibility for their change because you believe in them and yourself, your client's transformation will make them want to loudly proclaim their breakthrough, share what they're doing with others, and encourage them to join because it feels so good. Transformation commands clients to delve within themselves and be vulnerable to work on their issues (which can be scary), but when you are an authentic NBO who is leading your client, they feel like anything is possible, and they will be able to make bigger than ever jumps into empowerment.

Authenticity Engenders Trust

Your authenticity determines how deeply clients believe in you. The first thing clients look for is whether or not they like and trust you. Your authenticity is the bedrock of supreme sales skills. When working with clients, it is better to be inexperienced and authentic than to be experienced and inauthentic. Clients want a relationship with you. They want to trust you. They want to receive great service and transformation from you and proudly refer their friends to you. Think of how much we admire super-successful business owners who still can be authentic with us. We love them and want to keep them in our pocket, forever loyal. At no level of business does authenticity become unimportant. It is always important— more than clients, and more than your service. Always be as real, transparent and as honorable as possible with clients throughout your relationship with them, and they will reward you with their trust.

How Do Clients Choose Whom They Work With?

If a prospective client visits multiple practitioners like you, would they make a choice based on who they think does the best work? Or would they choose someone based on how good of a connection they feel with them?

When it comes to emotionally transformational work, trust is more important than credentials. Credentials may be a precursor, but a client's trust ultimately determines the sale. Clients who trust their own determinations won't need to see a list of credentials. Clients need to trust you to do deep, emotional work with you. In cultivating that trust, especially if you're in a service-related coaching field where emotional vulnerability is a factor, safety is key. You're in the business of empowering people. You do emotional work with them. So this book's sales system will cultivate your ability to build trust and client safety and security, and will guide you through asking those questions they need to answer before deciding to work with you.

Healthy Boundaries

What does it mean to have healthy boundaries with your client and protect your self-worth? Does it mean being cold and unfriendly? Not letting the client take advantage of you? Not giving in to your client when they have a bad experience working with you? Does it mean being a pushover or being firm? How can you use healthy boundaries to reach higher levels of professionalism so that you and your business remain safe and your clients are more inclined to invest in their transformation?

As NBO's, we each have our notions of what it means to maintain healthy boundaries with our clients. But we forget that many of us have people-pleasing and approval-seeking tendencies. It's human nature. These tendencies need to be kept in check when owning a business. Let's talk about how to exercise healthy boundaries and what maintaining them looks like in your business.

Client Friendships

I define friendships as spending regular social time outside the office where you may be inclined to emotionally and lovingly invest in each other. Having defined that, I recommend, as a general rule, that you be friendly, but not necessarily friends with your clients. This is especially a good rule to follow if you offer emotionally transformative services.

While authentic friendships can develop from working with clients, it's rare that they're long-lasting. Remember, the reason you attract clients is that you have something they need or want. This doesn't mean you can't be friends, but if you do pursue clients as friends, you must make certain that the friendship is reciprocal and equal. If your client is a fellow NBO, it's even better because they will be juggling the same challenges as you and therefore will be more likely to respect your boundaries.

Client friendships run the risk of the client taking from you, either consciously or unconsciously, if you or the client doesn't understand the distinction between your business and personal relationship. Often, the client will put you up on a pedestal, and you may be inclined to coach them outside of the office. This is bad for business.

If you are an NBO who has challenges with people-pleasing, know that people-pleasers tend to allow others to define their relationships. Allowing approval-seeking behaviors to be the foundation of your business is self-sabotage. You must be self-aware and not allow people-pleasing if you plan to be successful in business. Otherwise, you're likely not to develop professional confidence, not make much money, and have a social network of clients who have all turned into friends.

Inexperienced clients are going to want to bond with you. While this may be natural, be careful that it doesn't erode professional boundaries that you're intending to build. Many people create relationships based on how they please each other, but I don't recommend allowing that approach in your business because it's inauthentic. Clients who form relationships that way tend to have unstable boundaries and will enable themselves to feel entitled with you. Watch out for that because it's a form of manipulation. Don't get too casual.

Be friendly, but don't bend the rules for people who don't respect them. You can make exceptions occasionally when it feels right, but the rules and policies you create are designed to protect your business. Don't give clients the wrong impression about what working with you will involve. If you cut corners with your boundaries (rules, policies and seeking approval), you'll know because clients will show up late, cancel appointments, and treat you like they treat their friends. Instead, run your business how you envision yourself running it years from now. It's not going to be the end of the world if these things happen. Remember to identify these potential pitfalls and correct them early on. Don't be that NBO who is dealing with the same boundary issues, personal challenges and stuck at the same level of development many years from now.

Healthy boundaries are always going to be important with your client relationships, especially if you decide to "go big" and build a well-known brand. So I urge you to be alert for how some of your client relationships could be toxic now and you don't even know it, and correct them immediately. Set the standard for the NBO who you want to become.

Phone Texting with Clients

As much as possible, eliminate phone texting and online messaging with clients. I've watched my wife try to be helpful to clients who needed hand-holding outside of the office, only to watch them monopolize her time. Yes, my wife was getting approval from it and that's why she allowed it, but it escalated to her being completely not present at home because she was in constant communication with clients in her head during non-office hours because of the texting. Our time off wasn't time off. Her stress levels were constantly spiked at all hours of the day and night. It was a nightmare. Eventually, we had to cut off all client communication during non-office hours and have all of our clients phone the office or email when necessary.

Keep all client communications self-contained: phone, voicemail, email—but not texting or online messaging. Phone texting or any kind of rapid-fire online messaging can erode professional boundaries faster than a hurricane at Daytona Beach. Text messaging is more consuming and distracting than a phone conversation because phone conversations have a beginning and an end. Text messaging does not have a beginning and end; the mind spews text messages like a broken fire hydrant, and causes the recipient to be constantly mentally engaged and not present.

Not only is it healthy to unplug, texting sends the client the wrong message. It tells them that they can get more out of you, and it cheapens your work while lowering your self-worth. You think you're offering more, but you're offering less. Allowing yourself to get engaged with texting leads to coaching outside of the office and more. Texting is particularly difficult for NBOs because they are already people-pleasers, and people-pleasers allow others to define their relationships for fear of losing approval. If you know you are a people-pleaser, then you must practice firm boundaries, not only for the client, but also—most importantly—for yourself.

The best way to avoid getting drawn into the mire of out of office communications is to stay on time during your sessions. If clients want to talk to you when they're not in your office, either save it for the next session, have them send you an email or call your office phone and leave a message. Most office phone systems are accessible remotely if you need constant access. If online messaging is important to your business, at minimum, set office hours for when you will respond, but be disciplined.

Personality Types and Resistance Levels

Let's consider for a moment, personality types. I am an enthusiast of the Myers-Briggs typology system, and I've used it to help narrow down the archetypes in my clients' thinking processes. I highly recommend using Myers-Briggs in your practice as an assessment tool for your clients, especially if your practice has a coaching component.

You will find that most clients ultimately make buying decisions using their feelings. However, there are personality types who are "feeling-dominant" and "thinking-dominant." While this book is designed for NBOs who tend to be feeling-dominant and attract clients who are also feelers, once in a while, you will attract a thinking-dominant person. With dominant-thinkers, you may find that the process for reaching a non-verbal agreement takes longer or feels more awkward. (Non-verbal agreement naturally occurs when you've each determined that you feel no red flags, so you non-verbally agree to keep going forward in the process.) This is because dominant-thinkers associate more with their rational thinking processes. Therefore, they will likely ask questions about your credentials, experience and results. This isn't meant to be an insult to you. Dominant-thinkers will likely have higher resistance levels to vulnerability than dominant-feelers, and thus, require vetted, tangible trust symbols to compensate. Dominant-feelers will only need to know how they feel about you to trust you. This isn't black and white, and you will encounter many shades of gray within each personality because all people both think and feel. Nevertheless, I illustrate these personality archetypes to let you know that as a feeler NBO, when you encounter different personalities, it doesn't mean you are doing anything wrong. There is a lot you can do to educate yourself on how different people think and how you can engage them to increase your overall expertise.

Stay On Time

Even if you don't have another client afterward, stay on time! Dominant-feeler NBOs are more likely not to stay on time than dominant-thinkers. While feelers will have an easier time getting the client into their emotions than thinkers, your kryptonite (your Achilles heel) will be staying on time. If the client gets overly emotional into their story, a feeler NBO can get lost in that and think that it's time to do coaching during the Intake—please don't. *Don't mix coaching with an Intake Assessment.* Instead of responding to their story, ask your next Intake question. You need to focus on getting through your Intake questions on time. If you feel that you need more time for your Intake, you can use 30-60 minutes to give yourself wiggle room. There's no need to go over 60 minutes. 30-minute Intakes are mostly for high-volume practices.

Bonding with a client is not necessarily authentic. Bonding is good, but don't get emotionally involved. The client may misunderstand you and go into their story, and before you know it, you're coaching them. Let bonding be compassionately listening to their answers to your Intake questions while you are keeping your eye on the clock. Make sure you get through all of your Intake questions.

You can always give a quick answer anytime, but don't spend a long time on it. Redirect to another question about the client after providing a quick, satisfactory answer to their question. If answering their question would derail you, tell them you'll answer it shortly or at the end of the Intake.

Is Your Client Emotionally Accessible?

My business was hypnotherapy and emotional change-work, which required clients to get into their feelings for me to help them. It was essential to find out if those emotions were accessible before doing any work with them. That was one way I qualified a client's readiness to work with me. How open were they to talk about what was truly going on in their lives? Could they let down their defenses? Were they committed to their "why"? Were they committed to their dream? Were they committed to experiencing positive change? Or were they seeing me as a novelty? If they weren't emotionally accessible enough, I wouldn't try to work long-term with them because the deep emotional change-work is where I did my best work.

Dud Clients

Any client who's coming to see you will likely be in some form of victimhood because they were drawn to your emotionally transformative service. It's your job to qualify them. Are they in too much victimhood to work with you? Do they have too many victim behaviors to be accountable? Are they too closed off and inaccessible?

I look at dud clients as if they are on a scale or spectrum. At one extreme, you have dud clients who are so closed off that they are emotionally inaccessible and not ready to do emotionally transformative work. At the other extreme, you have dud clients who are so mired in emotional victimhood that they are unaccountable. In the middle, is a flexible range of clients who can be open enough and accountable enough to achieve transformation. Neither extreme client may be malicious or even aware they're doing these things, but both are instances where a client may not be ready to work, and you must qualify them so that you can politely and authentically disqualify them. There's no need to compromise yourself. The ideal client must be both emotionally accessible as well as accountable and taking responsibility for their change.

Watch out for people who claim that you are their "savior" or who are bad-mouthing someone else during your Intake, while being nice to you. These are victim clients. If a client is projecting hard judgments toward others, their behavior can eventually be directed at you. A well-conducted Intake Assessment should help to disqualify clients who would be bad for business. Clients with this much resistance are not likely ready for transformation. Use discernment. Don't blame yourself if you attract dud clients. It happens to every NBO, especially when starting your business. Every client is a gift that yields more clarity on the type of clients you want and you don't want.

Firing Clients

A client who cannot prioritize working with you into their life (despite their best intentions) means they are not fully committed to doing the work with you, and as a result, are not ready. The brain ranks everything based on emotional importance. If the client can prioritize your appointments, then you know they're serious about change. If clients don't complete your assignments or if they're not accountable in any other way, such as being consistently late for or canceling appointments, you're allowed to fire the client and give them a full refund, a partial refund or no refund. It's your decision. You don't have to struggle to help the client get results if they're not being responsible and accountable for doing the work with you. It's good to embrace clients who are ready to work, and it's also good to let go of clients who are not ready to do the work.

Turning Clients Away

When you are building your brand, don't try to help people who want something other than what you offer or who aren't ready for what you offer. My wife and I would politely and respectfully turn clients away regularly who weren't qualified to work with us. My wife turned one lady away, telling her that she wasn't ready, and that lady was so appreciative of my wife's honesty that she actually gave us referrals because my wife was authentic with her during her Intake Assessment and evaluation. Your authenticity is top priority.

Never Fix Clients

My wife would say to her clients, "This is your world, I'm just livin' in it." The client is running the marathon. Your job as an NBO is to run alongside them and hand them cups of water, supporting them in their journey. Never, at any point, should you give the client the impression that you are responsible for their transformation. You may offer a service, but the client must use what they learn and experience and *apply* it to their life. The client decides how deep, how fast and how long you will work together. If the client shows you they are responsible, accountable and puts into practice your guidance; they earn the privilege to work with you for the longer term.

Book Enough Time Between Clients

Never compromise the next client's session time because you're still working with the previous client. It's disrespectful to your clients, and it throws off your schedule. Give yourself ample time to finish with clients, rest if needed, and prepare for the following client. Once I was well-organized with my systems and had a receptionist taking the money and scheduling clients, I would see a maximum of seven clients per day. Depending on your type of service, you might see more or fewer clients. I would gain more momentum as the day went on, but my wife would need a break for an hour or two a couple of times a day to rest. Get to know what you need for rest and preparation, and give yourself enough time to get organized.

Chapter 3 Summary

- Your authenticity and client trust
- How clients choose whom they work with
- Setting healthy boundaries
- How clients' personality types effect their relationship choices with you
- What to do when clients aren't emotionally accessible

Chapter 4 - The Sales Mindset

The Master Salesperson

A master salesperson has total control of the sales process. She knows how to gently guide the client, find out what the client wants, qualify the client, politely dismiss a dud client (even if they're well-meaning), and connect with the client authentically. She does not pressure the client to buy. By the time she's done with the Intake Assessment, the right client will want what the master salesperson has and will have decided for herself that she likes her and believes she can help her. Sound too good to be true? It's not. I'm describing my wife.

No One Wants to Be Sold, But Everyone Wants to Buy

Have you ever heard the quote, "No one wants to be sold, but everyone loves to buy"? The phrase "no one wants to be sold" only means that they didn't feel good about buying what someone offered to them. "Everyone loves to buy" means they felt good about buying what someone had offered them. Feeling good is the difference. So how do we help people want to buy things? The key is to find out if they feel good about buying from *you.*

When qualifying your client, if you discover that the client is feeling good and you are feeling good, then after you've finished, the client will have virtually sold themselves. They felt good about you, so they wanted to buy from you. Selling doesn't mean doing things to people that they don't want to have done to them. Selling means coming to that place of feeling good and aligning together and letting the client decide for themselves that you are the right fit for them—then asking for the sale. Everyone wants to buy if they want the service and they feel that you are the right fit for them. Alternatively, if the client doesn't want or need you, there's no use in trying to interest them in what you have to offer.

Selling is about seeing as many people as possible to determine two things: whom you can help and if they want your help. If they neither want nor need your help, it doesn't mean you failed; you've succeeded in finding out whom you can help. Ask yourself how you can help the potential client connect with your solution if it seems they need you. It's about finding out if there's a genuine want or need from the client. It's about qualifying them, and that means asking the right questions. We'll get to those questions later in the book.

The Biggest Benefit in Working with a Lot of Clients

In working with more than 4,000 1-on-1 clients, what do you think is the biggest benefit that my wife and I have gained? Money? Experience? I would say experience. Experience is what you take with you to the next level. I don't only mean experience working with clients; I mean sales experience. If you stick with this, you will get so good at selling that the next natural step is going to feel like moving to a bigger playing field (eventually) where you are working with more clients at one time and selling bigger ticket items like group work and seminars.

On a similar note, your self-worth will grow along with your skill sets, your talents and your ability to sell. I recommend letting yourself expand into bigger avenues as this occurs. That might mean changing the way you do business or changing your industry or moving on to a completely different setting to reach more people. When you get good at catching a certain kind of fish with a certain kind of pole, it may be soon time to upgrade your pole to a fishing net. Sometimes, you won't have any more room for 100 small fish. You'll eventually gain the sales skills to catch one big fish to get the same amount of meat. Why do it a hundred times once you've learned how to do it better one time? Can you imagine riding a bicycle to work on an arduous commute after you've learned how to drive a car? It wouldn't make sense since your abilities have grown. A wellspring of lasting money comes from your ability to sell, and *your business will not outgrow your ability to sell.* Whatever happens, make sure you don't sell yourself short. Your business should always be a reflection of your ongoing personal growth.

Fear and Manipulation Tactics to Avoid

What are some things you've traditionally heard about selling? Do you think of the car salesperson? Are you afraid of coming across that way? Everyone fears being pushed or forced to do something they don't want to do. Let's talk about manipulation.

What is manipulation? Manipulation is getting people to do something that they are not aware of or wouldn't agree to. But better yet, what is the *fear* of manipulation? You're not afraid of manipulating; you are afraid of not being liked as a result of being perceived as a manipulator. Or, you're afraid of feeling guilty because you're trying to be successful. This is a commonly held belief that holds many people in check, especially NBOs, because they are already so in-tune with how others feel. The last thing an NBO wants to risk is being shunned by their tribe or professional circles. Thus, it's important to be as authentic as possible so that you genuinely set the example for business owners who come after you. This might be called social responsibility.

Social Responsibility

Socially responsible NBOs look out not only for themselves but also for their clients' best interests while setting a good example for others to follow. In contrast, non-socially responsible business owners would only be interested in looking out for themselves no matter who they negatively affect. Their motto would be: "Take all you can." It's good to adopt an abundant mindset, but not at the expense of eroding the social fabric. But don't worry. Not only would socially irresponsible business owners not pick up this book, but they'd also likely stop reading by now. When respect of self and others doesn't matter to the business owner, short-term wins may be high, but long-term detriments will eventually win out, in more ways than one. Do right by others, and they'll do right by you. Remember, a spiritual solution is one where both you and the client win.

Managing Client Expectations

Some clients may be stepping into an office like yours for the first time. They need to know they'll be safe throughout their experience. Knowing what they can expect is determined by how well you manage their expectations. You're not guaranteeing a specific result from your service, but you're transparent about what they might encounter throughout working with you.

Let nothing upset your client. If the client feels safe because your website has told them about your service, and you've told them what to expect (especially if doing emotional work), and if the client has the experience of exactly what you told them they might experience (within a certain range), then they'll feel *continually* safe. Instead of getting scared when their emotions come up during or after your service, the client will accept their experience as part of the process instead of reacting to it. They'll think, "Okay, she said I might feel this way while we do this emotional work, so I know this is normal, and nothing's wrong."

Clients want to feel that they're doing a good job. NBOs ask the client to be brave and vulnerable to create change, so when you share what they might expect to experience, they will not only feel safer, but they will also feel they're progressing and getting their money's worth. You are creating opportunities for the client to win when they reach various benchmarks and milestones you spoke of when you outlined your service. You'd be surprised how many clients are afraid of disappointing you for fear of not doing the transformation "right." Reassure them.

Whether in session, during the sale or before you meet the client, when you manage the client's expectations, you set up a framework and scope of how your service works. In essence, you're briefly explaining the structure of what you do: "here's what's going to happen; here's what you're likely to experience; here are the results you may get." Or, "here are the results that other people have gotten working with me."

Money Loves Structure

Every practitioner works differently, and you might not work as I do. I'm more of a structured person. You may not be. People love how grounded and confident I am when I work with them in session. My structured approach makes some people feel safe. If you are a non-structured person and more fluid, be sure you are still managing client expectations and staying on time. Since money loves structure, the more you can carve out what you do in words, on paper, video, audio and website ahead of time, the more people will be drawn to working with you.

I recommend explaining the majority of how your business works (its structure) via your online presence so that you can maximize your 1-on-1 time with the client in evaluating their needs. In person, you are still managing expectations as needed, but let your website and online presence do the heavy lifting.

Focus Your Services on What You Do Best

As a hypnotherapist and life coach, I can target many different issues clients face. At the beginning of my practice, I worked on *anything* the client wanted for fear of going out of business. It was a nightmare. In time, I noticed that I was better at servicing certain client issues more than others. I eventually made the wise decision to narrow my focus to working only on the issues that I was *best* at helping clients with and which I enjoyed. I eliminated working on the things that I didn't like or wasn't good at offering. The results were amazing. I felt better. I attracted more clients who wanted to do what I specialized in. I provided better results. I got more referrals and made even more money as a result. Don't try to help clients with everything; focus on helping with issues you're best at servicing and which make you feel good.

Tithing

If you want to give sessions to clients as a part of giving back, I recommend setting aside a specific number of sessions or clients to tithe to each month. We tithed one free session to two clients per month who genuinely couldn't afford our sessions but could benefit greatly from them. This was a one-time offering per client. Use your intuition to help you decide when or how often to tithe.

Bartering

In my experience, 99 percent of NBOs start off sharing their talents by bartering before receiving money for their services. Bartering is good for building confidence, but once you start seeing clients for money, I recommend saving bartering for strategic partnerships (non-client relationships) with other NBOs to help your respective businesses. Some instances may warrant bartering your service with a client who may offer your business a marketing service, for example, and I invite you to explore those possibilities as an NBO, but keep tabs on the energy exchange and performance of each person. You can barter by the hour or by the results. Evaluate the relationship regularly to ensure it's productive.

Chapter 4 Summary

- How to be a Master Salesman
- Fear and manipulation tactics to avoid
- How to manage client expectations
- Where to focus your services

Chapter 5 - Systems

Systems help you build a money pipeline instead of hauling pails of money each time. Every aspect of your business—from online Intake forms to price sheets—is a system and part of the sales process. Because I used systems, I began attracting a lot of people who wanted to do deeper transformative work. I discovered ways to use systems and processes to make selling easy and provide a ton of extra value, which made me passionate and my clients ecstatic. My clients wanted to be part of the energy my wife and I were creating. Walking into our clinic felt exciting. Instead of people hiding out in an antiquated therapeutic environment, clients would connect and be proud of their choice to have taken responsibility, knowing they were owning their change.

If you follow a healthy diet routine, you'll feel better and have more energy. Similarly, when you have a healthy routine in your business, you will have a better functioning business. Healthy routines in business mean using systems. Systems are tools that help you create routines intended to generate predictable and consistent results. If you deviate from using a system, you're going to get muddled results.

Systems Protect Your Self-Worth

When you create any system, you protect your self-worth. Here's a simple example of a system: a price sheet.

One piece of paper can be a system you use to protect your business. Your business can have many systems, from price sheets to calendars to contracts. When offering a sale, having your prices written down on a price sheet with your recommendations for service protects you from lowering your prices if you've had a bad day or if the client may be inclined to haggle your prices for a discount. You never want to evaluate your prices in front of a client. You should determine that before you see a client. If you give a discount, it should still not affect your bottom line. We'll talk more on that later in the book, but for now, you know to start using systems to help you stay accountable to your best thinking about your business while not succumbing to self-sabotage on your bad days.

Systems inform potential clients about the type of business you have before they set foot in your office. Having a client fill out a form online (avoid filling out in person to save time, if possible) with basic information saves you time. As soon as they start filling things out, you're already communicating the message that you mean business. Systems keep you on track, command respect from others, and save you time. Everything you ask a client to do before or during their work with you gives you an indication of how accountable they might be. Whether you take a naturally structured or unstructured approach to manage your business, systems will always protect your self-worth.

Expand Upon Your Biggest Returns

Have you heard of The Pareto principle? It states that 80 percent of the fruit your business produces will come from 20 percent of your efforts. What does this mean? If you make a list of your top-ten money producing activities in your business, more than likely, two of those ten activities will be responsible for creating the most amount of money. Therefore, figure out what those top two money producing activities are and prioritize them. Give those two activities the majority of your attention because they generate the most substantial returns. Similarly, when you don't know what to work on, make a list of ten and then focus on the top two that you think will produce the most benefit to your business. You may find that the other eight activities amount to busy work, with questionable productivity or effectiveness.

Did you know that Albert Einstein didn't know his phone number? When asked why, he said that he could look it up in the phone book to find it. He saved all of his brain power for his top 20 percent. Can you imagine how much time NBO's waste on social media? Don't clutter your mind with information you can find somewhere else. Be strategic in all your actions.

Systems Make You Effective

During my Intake Assessments (first client visit), I found that when I asked one of my key questions a certain way, it created confusion and clients would consistently reply, "What do you mean?" That part of my system wasn't working; I needed to reword that question. Once I did, I received no questions in return. I received the answers my question intended. I updated my Intake form system, and as a result, I saved time during *all* of my future Intakes. That one small change saved me a few precious minutes during my Intake Assessments and kept me punctual. When you're seeing 25-40 clients a week, as I was, a system change that saved me a few minutes per client made a massive overall difference.

Imagine if I had not used a system which contained specific questions to use. What if I had made up on the spot every question I asked during an Intake Assessment? One thing would be clear: I would have no basis on which to make improvements to my Intake Assessment. If I conducted it differently every time, how could I measure my effectiveness?

Two questions should qualify each business action an NBO considers:

1. Is my action an income producing activity?

2. Is my action automating my business?

Systems Automate Your Business

Anything that can assist you to automate your business is a system that makes you more effective. Do your work once and then make a system for it. Don't waste time re-creating anything that has already been created. Do the work once; decide what you'll do, then write it down. Create a price sheet, a vital information form, worksheets and sign-in forms. Use them repeatedly so that you have less to remember and you can focus on the task at hand. You can always update your systems as they improve. Have your systems in place so that you can focus on thinking about what the client is saying, and not trying to think about what you're going to say next.

Qualify Your Spending: Identify Needs vs. Wants

Before spending money on a system or tool that you think you might need, qualify your decision. Ask yourself if what you are considering is a "need" or a "want." More than likely, it is a want. For the majority of systems you will need to implement, you will be able to create them yourself (i.e., price sheets) or use for free (i.e., Google Calendar). I think the most money I ever needed to spend on a system consistently was $50 per month for a robust appointment scheduling calendar system that functioned per my customized needs. Other items included one-time purchases for office supplies and furniture.

A rookie mistake of NBOs is throwing money at problems and hoping for solutions. NBO's who don't scrutinize and qualify their business needs spend *a lot* more money than NBO's who do. Many NBO investments are bought on impulse, prematurely and without a strategy.

I once coached a client on systematizing her business, and we made great progress. But, she often fell victim to buying business programs and tools that were extremely expensive, unnecessary or ill-timed. Not only that, she bought them before she knew how to sell. I repeatedly tried to stop her, and it helped, but she didn't understand the following: having the greatest products didn't mean that clients would buy them. She was growing in debt, but not at becoming a more savvy business owner. Fortunately, she was offered a great job in another field that she loved, so everything worked out well for her. But, she incurred a lot of unnecessary debt. I think she now runs her business as a hobby for family and friends.

Qualify all of your business decisions. *Timing can invigorate or kill your business.* Ask for help in qualifying what you need from friends who are good with money or who are business coaches. Read books on the subject. Educate yourself. Track your income and expenses. Learn about sales and marketing and make sure you're checking your authenticity along the way. Practice using Microsoft Excel and watch some YouTube videos on it. There are thousands of hours of free trainings on YouTube on *anything* from beginner to expert level.

Considering how to grow your business is called strategic growth. If you do it properly, you can eliminate costly mistakes and grow your business faster. Be conscientious and frugal with how you spend your money in your business, even if you have a lot of money to spend. Practicing good habits will yield long-term gains and future wise business decisions.

Work On Your Business One Day Each Week

I recommend setting aside one day each week where you work exclusively on (not in) your business and its systems. On this day each week, you see no clients. You're only thinking about how to be more effective in your business. This could mean researching better methods online, reading business books, looking at your notes from client conversations and adjusting what you say to clients, updating price sheets and contracts. Working *on* your business day is when you reflect and make adjustments to improve, whether big or small. This is your day for measuring what you've been testing during the other days of your workweek. Look for trends. Test and measure everything, and have fun with it! This time can be deeply meditative and aligning to help you stay on track with your purpose. I know business owners who make millions who still work on their businesses one day each week.

Enlist Business Coaches and Mentors

At any stage in the game (and when you can afford it), I recommend working with a business coach whom you feel good about. You may start with courses online, but after a while, you will need 1-on-1 time for a coach to analyze your business needs and qualify your next steps. You will likely work with multiple coaches over time. The more successful an NBO becomes in business, the more coaches they will have. I heard one multimillion-dollar NBO state on her podcast that she has five coaches: business (two), wellness, finance, health. When you can't see your own limiting beliefs, having at least one business coach is imperative if you want to be successful as an NBO. Mentors are often business owners who tithe their services. You find mentors by building relationships with other NBOs. Mentors might not think of themselves as mentors, but you may identify them as mentors for you. Talk to them.

Give Your Clients Homework

Let's get into some examples of systems to use in your business. Many systems are often needed in business, but my favorite (and one of the most important) system to use in an emotionally transformative service-based business is giving the client regular homework. This system is important for client accountability, so we're going to spend some time on how to use homework as a system for your emotionally transformative service-based business.

At the beginning of my hypnotherapy practice, I felt that it was my responsibility to make sure the client was getting results. In time, I realized I was wrong. I was responsible for being authentic, supportive and providing the service, but I was not responsible for how deeply the client dove into their emotions to do the emotionally-focused hypnotherapy I provided. What do you think happened? The clients who took more responsibility and were more engaged, achieved better results. So I created a simple system to help all my clients take more responsibility—*I gave them homework.*

I gave them opportunities to engage. I created worksheets, assessments, and ways for them to go deeper without me. Not only did their results help me be more effective in helping them, but also, I could gauge how much of a priority my services were for them by whether or not they completed my easy homework assignments. I based this on trend. Did the client consistently complete the homework? Did she make an extra effort? Go above and beyond? Did he not do it at all? This homework-giving strategy taught me volumes about its importance. I never stopped giving homework throughout a client's life-cycle.

Giving the clients homework was an effective gauge in discovering their level of accountability. Future conversations with my wife about clients always involved the question: Are they accountable? Are they doing the homework? Are they canceling appointments? Are they showing up on time?

I always gave out homework, even before the sales pitch, and if clients didn't do the homework, I would often not offer to work with them long-term. This is one effective way to protect your brand and qualify your clients. You want all-star clients to define your brand who will later give 5-star Google Reviews. It's not only about the quality of your service, but it's also about clientele choices. Don't be afraid to give homework, even if you have a tarot card reading service. The vast majority of clients consider receiving homework a better value than your competitors who may offer less. Offering homework and other value add-on bonuses has been a primary reason I received so many referrals. If you're not sure about whether to take on the client, then assign homework and let their results do the talking.

Use Homework to Gauge Commitment Level

Homework helps make the client accountable, offers extra value—and most importantly—it gives you an indication of how your client is prioritizing their commitment to change, despite their other challenges.

Always give the client homework, especially when you are unsure about accepting the client on a long-term relationship. If they don't complete the homework you give them, you can ask why, and get a feel for what their obstacles and priorities are and work through them. You can identify non-accountable clients this way, and save yourself future headaches. It's never worth selling to a client who will buy but who isn't doing the homework because clients who aren't fully invested in their change may wind up not completing their sessions, self-sabotaging and asking for refunds.

There's No Such Thing as Not Having Enough Time

Everyone has 24 hours a day. If the client tells you they didn't have enough time to complete their homework, what they mean is that they didn't make it a priority. It's your job to determine the client's priority level and commitment level in your first conversation as best as you can. Homework helps the most with this. It only matters that the client completes the homework. How thoroughly the homework is completed isn't as important, but more thoroughly written homework responses (as opposed to one-word answers) will show more commitment. One word written responses are better than no responses at all. That's a big difference in psychological priority.

What Homework Looks Like

Your homework should be engaging, starting with filling out personal information (i.e., name, address, phone, personal details related to your business). Basic information should be completed before they see you. Assessments, paper homework, inventories, self-assessments, workbook exercises, buying herbal supplements, taking quizzes, reading handouts, watching a video or audio and reporting on it are all good types of homework. Make the homework engaging and provide value. It should take no longer than 5-10 minutes for the first couple of assignments. You can escalate the depth of the homework between sessions as needed.

Homework Provides Extra Value

Every time they put pen to paper, the client is psychologically committing a bit more, but more importantly, they are getting more value from you! The client will feel you want to invest in them when you give them homework. *If they didn't get homework elsewhere for the same service, they will feel they are getting a better value from you.* Show the client you are committed to their advancement even when they are not in the office by using homework. It shows you care about them even when they're not in the office for a session. How deeply you review the homework is up to you. You may also customize the homework, such as adding the client's name to the paperwork or personalizing some of the questions.

Using Online Forms

You might choose to use an online form to collect vital information. These should be "what" questions. These can include personal information like name and address, symptoms and medications. Save all your "feeling" questions for the first in-person visit; you need to ask these questions to the client. Also, never have the client fill anything out on paper in front of you during the first visit. If you need to collect vital information, make sure it occurs before your first visit starts so you have the client's full attention, even if that means starting the Intake Assessment late. I've rescheduled clients who didn't fill out my online forms before showing up for an Intake if filling those forms out in person meant I would not have enough time to conduct the Intake. If a traditional doctor needs vital client information before making an assessment, so do you.

Create a Price Sheet

Always print (don't write) your prices on paper. This includes your single sessions and package prices. When your prices are written down, you're less likely to negotiate your self-worth in front of the client, and you're less likely to be manipulated by hagglers.

In-House Coupons

In my hypnotherapy practice, we created a $20 in-house "coupon" and made similar offers on Groupon. This $20 coupon system included a free 30-minute Intake Assessment and a one-hour hypnosis session, all for $20. After both appointments were conducted (always on separate days), I would make session recommendations for clients and offer a sale at regular price. Through trial and error, I ended up doing it this way because hypnotherapy is experiential. Everyone has heard of hypnosis, but most people haven't experienced it. Conducting the Intake and allowing clients to get a taste of hypnosis built the incentive to buy a package. This is called creating a path of least resistance and having a low barrier to entry. You want to make it as easy as possible for your clients to say yes to working with you. If you feel that allowing clients to experience your service at low cost for their first session would build their incentive to work with you long-term, then try offering a $20 coupon which covers your Intake Assessment and the first one-hour session, then offer a package at the end of that first one-hour session.

Groupons

Groupon offers coupon deals for the public to try a variety of services or products from local businesses at low cost. Businesses primarily use Groupon as a way to bring in new customers with the hope of generating repeat business (https://www.groupon.com). Thus, the primary benefit of Groupon for NBOs is using it as a free marketing stream for lead generation. The low-cost coupons attract customers who might not be interested in non-coupon prices or who might not otherwise be able to find a small business due to Groupon's large exposure and customer-base. Businesses who host Groupons typically do not make a large profit from the Groupon purchases themselves, but from the opportunities to sell additional or longer term services and products to their customers. For service-based NBOs such as yourself, host Groupon deals to generate opportunities to sell after providing the Groupon service, *not* for making profit on the Groupon itself. If you create a Groupon deal, you will be required to see whoever buys the Groupon, but that doesn't mean you must sell your services to them.

You will have a maximum number of clients who will fill your schedule in a given week. You don't want to get inundated with too many coupon-holding clients per week, so you'll want to add some expectations (terms and conditions) in your Groupon deal to ensure clients know they won't get seen within hours of buying the coupon. Save space for sales opportunities. I recommend seeing two

Groupon Intakes per day to allow your schedule to gradually fill up, and save the rest of the slots for service sessions.

Nineteen dollars was the ideal price that created many Groupon sales when I used it. Also, I recommend putting a limit on the number of Groupons you allow to be purchased in a specified timeframe when running your deal. Find out how many clients you can see per week. Assume that 30 percent of your Groupon responders will redeem immediately, 30 percent will take weeks or months to redeem, and 30 percent will wait until the 6-month deadline to redeem at the last minute or not redeem at all.

Value Add-On Bonuses

Clients love to receive something tangible when they make a service package purchase, so including a physical item, like a homework workbook, or even digital items like MP3s or videos you've created will add more value in the client's eyes. These value add-ons tell the client what they'll receive at the time you offer the sale in addition to your service, which will exceed their expectations, make the client happy, and promote the package sale.

If you're an author with published books, include them as value add-ons (or even as homework). This can present more credibility for the sale, in addition to the trust you've already built with the client. Remember, the major qualifier of a value add-on item is that you're not giving more of your *time* away. The value add-on item must be a product you've already created and can distribute to all clients.

It is crucial that you never lower your prices for a client below your lowest feel-good price. If you feel tempted to lower your prices for a client, offer a value add-on instead. When you use the value add-on incentive, the clients get more value, and you are not risking the client seeing *your* value as less worthy. Always offer value add-ons instead of lowering your prices past what you've determined. If the client *still* doesn't see the value after you've offered the packages and value add-ons, I recommend saying, "Sorry, this is the best I can do. Take it or leave it." If the client leaves, allow them to leave. Your business has concluded.

One time, I wanted to give a client a discount because I liked her so much—big mistake in my self-worth. This client was such a great example for me because when I offered the discount to ensure she'd work with me, she said, "Don't lower your price for me!" She was one of the best clients I ever had because she taught me that I should never lower my price to be worthy of a client receiving what I had to offer. More worth means more money!

Get Google Reviews

One of the best systems you can implement is setting up your "Google My Business" account for free. This allows identification of your business on Google Maps. Enter your business information so potential clients can find you. Once it's set up, begin collecting authentic Google Reviews from your all-star clients, and ask them to be transparent about the transformation they received from you, if they are comfortable doing so. If you are being proactive with this, limit one review per week so that Google does not get suspicious about "review stuffing." The best practice is to put forth a consistent effort to encourage clients to leave Google Reviews organically. Potential clients will find your business and read your former clients' reviews.

The Google Reviews strategy brought in more high-quality clients and more money than any other system. This is a must-do. After a couple of years, when I asked new clients what made them decide to choose us, the majority of them said, "I read the Google Reviews." My former clients' Google Reviews attracted my new clients. In addition, the more reviews you get, the better your business will rank on Google because Google will trust your business more with consistent reviews. I recommend having at least 20-30 Google Reviews. (Yelp is also good, as long as the client is an active Yelper.)

Office Space

As a client, do you think you'd be willing to make a bigger investment in your transformation if the healer you visited had an office space? NBOs who have office spaces are seen as more credible. Your office space is a major system and income producer. If your clients arrive to your office for the first time and see a professional lobby with a front desk and receptionist, they immediately know you are legitimate. A reception area where clients gather is a form of social proof, and makes clients feel safe when they see other clients. I recommend using a client "sign-in" sheet at the front desk. Systems like these position (or "posture") the client for the sale before you even offer it.

If you're working out of your home, make sure your space looks professional. Before you rent an office space, it would be wise to master this book's content to ensure you are capturing as many sales as possible before taking on the significant expense of office space rental.

With each passing year, more wellness centers pop-up, operated by NBOs. Do some Google searching, make some phone calls, and chances are you'll be able to find a professional space with like-minded NBOs to discuss space rentals. Many of these NBO centers rent by the hour or have informal contracts (which are ideal). These finds are great for community, networking, and referrals. Renting your own office space does not have to be difficult and you don't have to do it alone. There are many other NBOs who are doing or want to do what you're doing.

If you're "going it alone" and not renting hourly, before you sign and lock yourself into a formal office lease, make sure you have a regular stream of paying clientele, and most importantly, make sure you know how to sell. Don't sign a formal lease for more than six months to one year at a time. Wait until your business is overflowing with clients so that the numbers justify your expansion. I've seen countless NBOs make unqualified, impulse business decisions, only to close their doors or severely scale back within a few months.

Merchant Services

Clients won't pay hundreds of dollars in cash. Merchant services allow you to securely accept debit and credit cards. Traditional merchant services are designed for high-volume businesses, charge substantial per transaction fees, and sometimes have an annual fee. Fortunately, many phone apps now accommodate lower volume needs, and many don't have transactional or annual fees. When researching, I recommend that you qualify them by their security, fees and positive user reviews.

Chapter 5 Summary

- What are Systems?
- How Systems protect your self-worth
- How Systems make you effective
- Applying the 80/20 rule
- Managing your spending
- Tips to strengthen your strategies and attract clients
- Adding value to your services

Chapter 6 - The Sales Process

The Big Three: What You Should Focus on When Selling

Focus on three things when selling: *asking key questions, engaging the client emotionally, and listening compass-ionately.*

Clients make appointments with you because they want to feel better. You know what it's like to face the world. It can be stressful. Families, jobs, friends and obligations can weigh heavily, and most people do not make their self-care a priority. People sweep their feelings aside all the time. It is a biological fact that our bodies don't register pain consciously until we are feeling at least 90 percent pain subconsciously. Some clients are so disconnected from their pain, they may not even remember why they made the appointment. If the client doesn't connect with what they feel inside, they remain victimized to their defenses operating in the background, sabotaging themselves from receiving your help.

You *must* get the client out of their head and into their heart. When you ask key questions and compassionately listen, you are engaging the client emotionally, and genuinely caring about them. Caring helps the client give himself permission to receive from you, get centered and reconnect. This helps the client release some stress and feel emotions. Just like you are working on how to receive, so are your clients.

Your questions invite the clients to look deeper within themselves and feel the truth about their current state so they can emotionally reconnect with why they made the appointment. You are assisting them to feel safe enough to bring to the surface what they feel so they can take a true self-inventory and explore with you why they need your help.

As you focus on the Big Three, you naturally qualify the client. This means you acquire the information you need to determine if you will work with the client. This also helps the client to self-qualify; to determine if they are in the right place, willing to be accountable and emotionally ready to engage.

You Need to Remind Them Why They Came to See You

If the client doesn't emotionally connect with why they came in, it may be because they have dismissed their problem; it isn't important because it's not staring them in the face at that moment. But you and I know that the problem is still there and that it is likely tied to much deeper issues and the client is only experiencing a small part of it. Ninety percent of anyone's problem is subconscious, with only ten percent of the issue occasionally coming up to break the surface of one's awareness.

Most people don't know what they're feeling until they break down, especially if they like to run from their pain instead of facing it. They need you to care, to be present, to check in with them and ask them what's going on. Watch your client carefully to see whether or not they're responding authentically to your questions. If you're being authentic, you can determine if they are willing to be authentic so they can receive your help.

Once you do ask the key questions, the clients who are least likely to run from themselves will allow themselves to feel what's going on and become transparent, showing you their emotions. When that happens, you can be assured of two things: 1) the client trusts you enough to be willing to become vulnerable, and 2) that makes them a potentially good client to help. Vulnerability and transparency do not mean the client needs to cry during their first visit. Not everyone cries, and your job isn't necessarily to break them down. But as long as you're seeing an openness and a willingness from them, you're in good shape.

Lead Them Through a Process

How clients answer your key questions is not as important as the psychological process you are leading them through. You should write down what they say, but more importantly, you should be monitoring how much the client is emotionally engaging. Are they becoming immediately emotional? Are they not emotional enough? Since your key questions will be printed on your Intake sheet (with room for interview notes), you will have the latitude to determine yours and the client's authenticity.

57

This is crucial. You are not only monitoring their ability to be vulnerable, but you are also observing and feeling how comfortable *you* feel as they speak. You are looking to build momentum from the amount of depth, transparency, connection and trust you both feel.

Key Questions First, Explanations Second

Always ask your key questions before you explain the details of your business. The details of your business should only be explained as a supplement after the client has already emotionally bought into your service after you've completed your key questions. The explanations and details of your business (the "what" questions) should be available to your client online before they see you in person. When you schedule the client, encourage them to review the details about your business online before their first in-person visit. The in-person visit is reserved for "why" questions, which are your key questions.

NBOs tend to over-explain what they're selling, or they give explanations instead of asking key questions. When you over-explain, the client is leading you with their questions. Don't allow that. Most explanations of how your business works will go right over the client's head, so never lead a client's first visit with explanations. Stick with your key questions. *When the client asks questions about how your business works, they are trying to cultivate trust about you, but you do not want them to manage that process. Your key questions will cultivate the trust they're looking for.*

Many NBOs think that clients are going to buy based on whether or not they understand the details of your service. It's natural to want to explain to get your point across. But people don't buy emotionally transformational services based on mental assessments. They buy based on feelings.

Asking the key questions will create buy-in and emotional engagement from the client, and after they are engaged and on-board, then you can explain the structure of how your service works—if needed. You may not need to explain your service, but you do need to ask key questions.

Who's in the Driver's Seat?

The person who asks the questions leads the way. Your sales process will have gone smoothly if you are asking the majority of the questions, and the client is answering them. If the client starts digging in with repetitive questions, and you find yourself constantly explaining, you're no longer in control. Over-explaining leads to you defending yourself. It's okay for the client to ask for clarification from you, but it's not okay for the client to drive. If the client thinks it's okay for them to drive, that means they think they are in control and can take advantage of you, if they so choose. But they are not in control—you are.

Why shouldn't the client try to control? If the client is controlling, then they are not *emotionally engaged*. The first visit is then rendered useless. Since your line of questioning is most important, asking the right questions gets the client emotionally vulnerable and involved with the process. Then they can identify what they're feeling and why they need your services.

When You Should and Shouldn't Sell

I've pursued working with clients who told me they were interested in working with me, but they were speaking from their heads, not their hearts. I hadn't reached their "why." Granted, I was excited about their desire to work with me, but my gut wasn't onboard. I hadn't connected with them. Can you guess what happened? They fizzled out. They ended up backing out of working with me. They weren't committed. They wanted a quick fix.

Don't solely rely on what the client says. A classic example of what to avoid is the client who is super-stressed and desperate, but they mask their stress with fake excitement, which is inauthentic. This could be a good client, but you will not know for sure until you've conducted a proper Intake Assessment on their first visit and helped them connect with their feelings and the pain under their defenses. You need to recognize (and you might even be able to feel) when a client is in lying behaviors. This means they're not being truthful because they're in fear. You can't do transformational work with someone who's in denial.

Sell when you feel good in your gut, and it matches what you're hearing the client say. If you don't feel good in your gut and the client is giving you "yeses", the client is in a lying behavior, and not acting with integrity or in alignment with what they're saying to you.

You don't need to invest significant time and energy if your gut is telling you that the client isn't a good fit, even if they're saying yes to you. If you are feeling good about the client, and the client feels good—even if they aren't giving you yeses—that's a better indication of working with them than yeses, which come from lying behaviors. Always go with your gut feeling. There is more intelligence in your gut feeling than what your brain can analyze from words.

Most of your non-sales will be for the following reason: the client bought into their expectations before you helped them reach their emotional reasons for seeking your services. Posture the client correctly via your systems and online presence before they come into your office for the first time.

Schedule Sales Opportunities During Your Peak Performance Hours

Some NBOs are morning people; others are more awake in the evening. You know when your most productive hours are. Schedule your clients during those hours. More specifically, schedule your sales opportunities during those times when you have the most energy. Between the hours of 2pm and 4pm, my wife could sell a ketchup popsicle to a woman in white gloves. I made the most sales between 5pm and 7pm. As a result, we deliberately scheduled sales opportunities during the hours when we felt the best, which coincided with the hours where we made the most sales.

Chapter 6 Summary

- What you should focus on when selling
- How to determine if you will work with the client
- Working through client resistance
- Maintaining control of the process
- When you should and shouldn't sell

Chapter 7 - The Intake Assessment In Depth

At the Intake Assessment you ask your key questions, and it's the most important system in your business. Think about it: we're spending many hours together in this book focusing on how to think about and conduct a process that essentially takes 30 minutes. Let's continue.

Why You Must Conduct a Free 30-minute Intake Assessment (and Do it Correctly)

In the last chapter, we covered the client's lying behaviors. The Intake Assessment invites the client to get out of lying behaviors so that you can discover if they're ready to be authentic with you. Only then, can you entertain working together.

You want to perform your best work so that your clients can achieve their best results. But long-term transformation doesn't occur in one session. You need a more robust sales method that allows you to do your best work. You protect your self-worth by having an Intake System that clearly explains to potential clients how long they can expect to work with you to get desired results.

In most cases, a client's desired result requires more time than he or she may realize. The client is coming to you for change, and you know what their change will require— if they are willing to be accountable. Before you ask for a financial commitment, you need to qualify and build trust with your client and evaluate how much time *you* need to produce *your* best results. By implementing the Intake Assessment, you will find out if working with a client would serve both you and the client and, if so, make recommendations and sell packages of sessions to achieve desired results.

If you are selling an emotionally transformative service that requires a long-term investment to achieve long-term results, then you'll need time to sell them on the long-term benefit of investing in your service. Transformational services are not an immediate gain. Healing an emotional trauma isn't a one-stop-shopping experience. To sell a client on long-term results, I use the 30-minute Intake Assessment.

The Intake Assessment is for Evaluation Only, Not Coaching

Never give the client the impression that you're going to do healing work with them during your Intake. Many clients are struggling with emotional well-being and are generally ready to allow anyone—*anyone*—who's willing to listen to help them. If your client starts getting emotional and going into "therapy mode" during the Intake, telling you their story, you must curb that right away. Don't let the client go on for more than 5 minutes. They may tell their story when you ask the first Intake question, "What do you want?" Approximately 20-30 percent of my clients would engage the therapy mode during the Intake and expect me to coach them. *Do not allow it.* This is not what the Intake is for. Step back and say that you understand and empathize without coaching. You can tell them things like, "Thank you for telling me that. We can work on that if you find that working together is a good fit, but let's go ahead and move onto the next question." Do not start coaching them at any time during the Intake.

Use the Same Intake Questions with All Clients

When you use the same questions for every client, it allows you to 1) focus on the client's responses and respond meaningfully to them, 2) know how well the questions are working as a trend among all your clients, and 3) take notes after each response.

You shouldn't be thinking about what to ask a client during an Intake—*ever*. Your questions are always predetermined and they should be doing all of your work for you so that you can focus on your intuition, your client's responses and their body language. Let your predetermined questions do the heavy lifting.

Stick to Your Timeframe

When I first got started in business, I didn't know exactly how to conduct an Intake properly, but I knew that the first visit with the client was important. Initially, I was in the process of discovering which questions were important to ask during an Intake. My natural skill was that I was good at noticing what worked and didn't work and made course corrections (testing and measuring).

At first, it was easier to conduct the Intake in 30 minutes because I wasn't deep-diving with the client to discover if I could help them do long-term transformative work. I wasn't confident enough to offer deep, transformative work; I wasn't even sure how deeply I could help the client create transformation and lasting results.

After seeing about 1,000-2,000 clients, my 30-minute Intakes would average about 45 minutes because that was the most natural amount of time that allowed me to cover everything I wanted to cover. It became an effective rhythm or flow for me. As my business evolved, I felt that 30 minutes was rushed because I was eventually selling bigger packages of sessions and that required me to go deeper on my Intakes with my clients.

As you begin, you might find that you can conduct your Intakes in 30 minutes. If you find you need more time, that's fine. Make sure you set the expectation with the client. Don't tell the client the Intake will be 60 minutes if you might do it in 30 minutes or vice versa. I eventually told my clients that I offered a free 30 to 60-minute Intake. If you give a range of time and stick to it, both you and the client know that you stuck to your offer of a 30-60 minute Intake, and the client will gain more trust (or professional respect) in you.

Book the Intake and First Service Session on Different Days

Always make sure that your 30-minute Intake and your first service session are scheduled on different days, 1-3 days out, but no more than a week. If the client is coming from out of town, then you can schedule them on the same day for both appointments. In my business, I determined that if a client had to drive longer than an hour, I would allow them to make both appointments in one day. Through testing and measuring, I found that booking these two appointments on separate days created the best results. The time lapse gets clients excited due to the possibility of creating change, they read more on my website about me and hypnotherapy, they speak to their spouses about their desire to do this work and perhaps secure funds, and most importantly, I give them homework to do and bring back. Since my service packages were hundreds and up to a thousand dollars or more, giving the client time to reflect upon their thoughts and desires helped them justify the purchase. You can experiment with other approaches, but this 2-day and 2-appointment approach worked best for my business.

Session Lengths and Check-Out Times

When I conducted an hour-long first service session (after the Intake day), I would save 10-15 minutes for offering the sale at the end of the hypnosis session. You need that time to do the following: 1) Offer the sale and allow the client to choose a package, 2) have the client pay, 3) give them homework, and 4) book them for the next session. Clients didn't mind stopping early, especially if their first service session was for $20. If you want to do a full hour session, that's fine. Make sure you give yourself at least 10 to 15 minutes after that first service session to complete the above steps and rest if you need to rest before your next client.

Anytime Questions

Let's review a few sample Intake questions and explore what they're used for. You may experiment with any of these questions that feel the best to you. (Later, I will share my favorite questions.) You may find yourself naturally re-wording these to suit your style and bring you better results with testing and measuring.

"What do you think?"

You can ask this one in the beginning, in the middle or after you've offered the client your price sheet.

"Do you see a benefit to that?"

This could be a clarifying question. This is a yes or no answer, which can be good for finding out where the client stands and whether it's time to proceed to the next step or determine if you need to take a step back.

"Would you like my help?"

This is a straightforward and easy way to ask for the sale after you've shown the client your prices.

"Do you have any questions?"

I save this one for use toward the end of the Intake because I know that, at the beginning of the Intake, they will have a lot of questions. If the client starts firing off questions early on, I ask them to hold their questions until the end because I will have answered many of them by the time I've finished the Intake. By the time I've finished, the client has virtually no more questions. This typically means that you've successfully taken the client through an emotional process. You've asked the right questions and they've opened up to trust you.

As you sharpen your Intake, you will be answering their questions naturally before the client asks them. But don't leave them behind. Make sure they stick with you as you are speaking. Look for head nods, and affirmative responses. If you're not getting them, slow down and ask questions to re-engage and ensure they are on the same page with you. If they have no questions at the end of the Intake and they're generally smiling and affirming, you're doing things correctly.

Trial Closing Questions

These are sample questions that help you figure out if it's time to start closing the sale. These are great to ask to make sure the client is following you through the Intake and to address any potential objections before closing the sale.

"So what do you think of "x" benefit?"

"How does that sound so far?"

"How do you feel about this service? Does it makes sense to you?"

"Did I miss anything?"

"Do you like it?"

"Could you see yourself in this program?"

"Let's put aside the price. Would this be the right service for you?"

"Feel, Felt, Found" Method

After you use the trial closing questions, you can experiment using the "Feel, Felt, Found" method: "I understand how you feel; others have felt the same way; here's the solution we found."

Closing Questions

These are questions you can experiment with after the Intake questions are complete and all of the trust-building has been done.

"Do you believe this solution meets your needs?" (If you get answers other than "Yes," you need to follow with, "Why not?" and then address the observed objection, then re-close.)

"Is there anything else you need to know about this service?"

"Is this what you were looking for?"

"Does what I'm offering solve your problem?"

"Would you like this package or that package of sessions?"

Todd's All-Star Intake Assessment Questions

Here are the fundamental points I've been leading up to. These are the exact key questions I have asked over 4,000 clients because they create predictable results, and I strongly recommend you use them during your Intake Assessment if you see clients live 1-to-1 in an emotionally transformative service-based business. I recommend you copy them down and use them on one sheet of paper (a system) where you leave spaces to write in client answers. You don't need to include the explanations in parentheses on your worksheet.

"What made you decide you wanted to come see us? What do you want? Why?"

(Purpose: opens rapport, provides clarity; limit their story to 2-5 minutes max)

"How will you know when you got what you came for? What will you see, hear, feel?"

(Purpose: future-pacing, identifies the result so they know what it will feel like when they've arrived.)

"What are you getting out of staying in this situation and choosing not to change?"

(Purpose: helps them identify why their current situation is not where they want to be. Builds incentive to change.)

"What's stopping you from having what you want? In what way?"

(Purpose: helps them get ultra-specific and self-identify with the roots of the issues as they know them; identifies pain-points. If they answer "Me," follow with, "In what way?")

"If you don't address these issues, what will your life look like in a year?" (Health / family / relationships / finances)

(Purpose: helps them self-identify what their life will look like if they *don't* change and how bad that could be; builds incentive to change. Emotions may arrive by now.)

"What resources or strengths do you have, or might you need to create these changes?"

(Purpose: helps them define solutions; gets them into problem-solving mode after you've broken new ground.)

"Teach me how to have the problem you're currently having. How did you arrive here?"

(Purpose: helps them show you what they think their problem is attached to in their mind.)

"How committed are you to making these changes? (Use a scale of 1–10 here, then ask "Why?")

1 2 3 4 5 6 7 8 9 10

(Purpose: If you've conducted the previous questions correctly and engaged them in a process where they access their feelings, you may already know the answer. This question affirms their position and commitment. If their answer is 5 or less, you need to find out why and address it.)

Close the sale

You can now begin with your closing question(s) if you wish. Or say, *"I'm going to make some recommendations for you based on our time together today."* Then offer your session package recommendations (price sheet) for them written on paper. Then offer it to them and be quiet until they respond.

Try different approaches with your Intake questions and closing questions and see what works best for you. These Intake questions and the client's payment can be done in 30 minutes.

Chapter 7 Summary

- The most important system in your business
- Why you must conduct a free assessment
- Setting standards and sticking to them
- Encouraging client participation and engagement
- Which questions to ask the client and how to ask them

Chapter 8 - Closing the Sale

We need to extrapolate some important points and scenarios that may occur when closing the sale, so I've devoted a chapter for it. Let's begin.

Always Ask for the Sale

Never forget to ask your customers for the sale. You don't know if they're going to buy or not buy. Unless your gut is telling you not to work with this client, you must ask for the sale. Even I didn't always know whether or not a client was going to buy. That's why I always used my Intake process. I never wanted to make assumptions. When I've deviated or skipped steps or questions, I've lost the sale in my overconfidence. Don't get cocky, don't be meek and don't assume anything. If you feel uncomfortable asking for money, your client will feel uncomfortable giving you money. Follow the system, and ask for the sale. If you find that anything in your sales process isn't working, then you need to go back, reread earlier chapters and practice.

After You Ask a Closing Question, Be Quiet

After the client has gotten into an emotional process and they've given me affirmative answers along the way, I'll either recommend a range of sessions for what I think they need or I'll give them one recommendation. I'll circle my recommendations on the price sheet and present it to them. Then I'll ask, *"Which one feels best to you?"* Or, *"Which one sounds good to you?"* Then I'll shut up and give them a good 20-30 seconds to answer. The client is now staring at the price sheet I created. They're not looking at me. They're looking at the paper with prices written on it. *Do not* explain any more at this point. You must wait for them to answer. The client will say things like, "I want to do the 12-pack of sessions, paid in full." Or, "I want to do the 6-pack paid in full (or payment plan)." They'll pick from your price sheet with packages written on it that you recommended.

Don't Forget Your Value Add-ons

When you make your package recommendations, don't forget to tell the client the value add-on bonuses they *will* receive for being a package client. I found it was a good idea to put these value add-ons on a separate sheet beside the price sheet and verbally walk them through the value add-on bonuses.

When the Client Doesn't Answer

There will be times when the client will get stuck in fear, and they don't know what to do or are unwilling to commit. *Only* after 20-30 seconds, it's okay to ask some follow-up questions to pinpoint their hesitation. *"What are you thinking?"* Or, *"What are you feeling?"* Get them to talk. Then you can find out how much fear they have about money, how much they can afford, and if you need to downgrade to a smaller package of sessions to get started.

What to Do and Not Do If They're Indecisive

When a client says they don't have the money to buy, it's rarely true. In my experience, what they most likely mean but won't say out loud is: "While I do have some money, it's not a priority for me to spend it on your service." They may have more fear than desire to move forward, or they may not want what you offered. If the client has more fear than desire at this point, then you need to practice your Intakes. Case in point: when you feel great about the client, and vice versa, and money is still an issue for them; you will both find a way to make your pricing work. If the client wants to move forward with a package but they're still skittish, opt for a smaller pay-in-full package as opposed to a larger payment plan package.

If you are nearing the end of your scheduled time, and the client still has questions, you can suggest to have them buy one session (as opposed to a package), or email you their remaining questions and follow up. But don't fall into the trap of trying to convince the client to buy if they're indecisive. Respect your own time (even if there's no client scheduled after the client you're speaking with right now). Don't give up control of the situation. If a client is not moving closer to buying and the clock has run out, I strongly recommend telling them, "It sounds like the timing might not be right for you to get started, and our 30-60 minute Intake is up. Would you like me to follow up with you in a few days with a phone call or email?" Regardless of the outcome, stop your session on time. *Stopping your session on time sends a bigger message of self-worth while posturing the client than anything you could say.* Leave it at that. The clock isn't your enemy; it's your friend to maintain self-worth.

If Money Were No Object

If you've asked the client, "Which option feels best to you?" and you've presented the price sheet to them with your packages on it, and the client hasn't responded for 20-30 seconds, they are likely either figuring out how to say no or how to pay for it.

If a client has indicated that they want to work with you and they're not 100 percent sure how they're going to pay for it, you can always ask the client which package they'd choose if money were no object. Ninety-nine percent of the time when you ask this question, they're going to tell you which package they want to buy.

When looking at your price sheet, if the client shows interest in a session package, but voices a legitimate money concern, ask them the following:

"If money were no object, which of these packages would you want?"

It's a fantastic question to use because asking it reveals the client's true desire for working together if money wasn't a factor. Most of the time, the client will say, "Well, I would definitely do the 'x' package of sessions." When you have that answer, you are virtually done selling. All you need to do then is find a way to help the client finance it. You can create and offer any number of payment plans, and I recommend you create payment plan and pay in full contracts with auto-debit payment dates with a refund policy of your choosing. (You can Google examples.) I will say that it is generally better to do a pay-in-full small package than finance a big package if money is a concern.

Don't Lower Your Prices

If the client still has more fear than desire to move forward at the end of the Intake—it's not your fault. You haven't done anything wrong. You can give additional options to the client if you want, as in a smaller package or a single session, but do not—I repeat, do *not*—lower your prices if the client is still in *fear*.

If you lower your prices for clients who are still in fear and victimhood at the *end* of your Intake (and not feeling empowered and hopeful as intended), it means you still have low self-worth in business. It's when the client's victimhood convinces you to get into your victimhood. Don't commiserate as victims together. That's a trap. Your business needs to uplift both of you to the next level. If it doesn't, then you're *both* falling into old patterns. You're here to break the client out of their old patterns, not allow the client to pull you into yours. By lifting them, you lift yourself! This scenario is one example of running a limited, fear-based business versus a business that raises you and your clients up to the next level.

Instead of discounting your prices, offer value add-on incentives. Give them MP3s, e-Books and other valuable supplements you've created. This means they're getting more from you while not minimizing your value. This is a *huge* distinction. If you were to lower your prices, you'd be sending the message that the client can haggle, victimize you and stay in control. How can you convince the client that you're able to help their self-worth when you're demonstrating that you still struggle with yours? You do no one a service by lowering your prices. Instead, give them an incentive to step up with your value add-on incentives. Clients are more inclined to buy when you give them something extra on top of what they were already considering buying. Last, make sure your value add-ons do not commit more of your *time* with the client. Make sure the value add-ons are duplications of yourself: MP3s and videos.

As you become more skilled at selling, you will attract ideal clients as a result of your increased self-worth. Clients will want to buy what you're offering because they want your confidence! Even when they don't have the money, they'll find the money! If people are finding money to work with you, it means you are headed in the right direction in your business.

If They Want to Think About It

When you offer your prices and your client says, "Can I think about it?" it means you didn't properly qualify them or they have unaddressed concerns. If they have interest in a package, a good practice is telling them that they need to put some money down today to take advantage of a discount before they leave, even if only $100. When I offered that, some clients wouldn't go for it, but some clients jumped at the chance to pay $100, get the discount, and pay the rest later (and they did). If they could invest in the package price, then I knew they were serious. If they couldn't, then I knew that "thinking about it" meant they weren't interested, and that was okay. Experience also taught me that extending a discount for 24 hours rarely made a difference in their buying decision. If the client says they have to "talk with someone" or "check their finances" and they don't immediately follow that statement with asking questions about how to start working with you after they do their "checking," I guarantee they're not going to buy or come back. That's their polite way of avoiding saying no. It's fine; just let them go.

Free Sessions

I only recommend offering a free session to a client when you know you've made a substantial mistake, and the client is *not expecting* a free session. If the client is expecting a free session, and you give them one, then they know they can manipulate you. Free sessions may ease tensions, but they cheapen your work. Even with your best intentions, free sessions send clients the wrong message, so try to avoid using them.

If They Don't Want a Package of Sessions

If you have a business, like hypnosis or tarot card reading that's often publicly identified as a novelty, then you need to offer your serious clients single sessions in additional to packages. I recommend that every NBO offer single sessions regardless of public perception. Your price sheets should have a single session price along with your package prices. Remember, the Intake isn't only for selling packages; it's for qualifying the client so that you can find out if you want them and how much they need you.

Selling vs. the Sale

The selling happens during the Intake Assessment, but the actual sale (money exchange) happens after your first session. Most clients will internally decide if they will work with you during the Intake, and this is what we want because our key questions draw out the sale. But, I recommend you pitch the package sale only after you complete the first discounted or full price session. This way, the client can pay for only one session if they don't want to do long-term work with you. Either way, you have properly postured the sale and set yourself up for success.

Alternative Ways to Close the Sale

I don't recommend this, but there are alternative options to asking for the sale. You could hire a receptionist to accept payments after you've rendered an Intake or service (although this gives your client wiggle room to back out if you haven't properly qualified them). You could have your client pay you online before or after your session (after is not ideal). You could work as an employee or partner with another NBO and perform your services in a capacity where you don't have to sell or handle money.

If you consider implementing the above options, I must warn you that you will lose more money than you intend to make and will also negate the self-worth you are building right now. With the knowledge you've gained thus far, choosing not to close the sale yourself would be like running a full marathon but refusing to cross the finish line. It may seem inconsequential not to ask for the sale yourself, but as an NBO, I promise—it is detrimental. Asking for and accepting money yourself is crucial to your self-worth development. If you are considering using these alternative ways to close the sale, consider going back and rereading the first two chapters of this book on self-worth, and practice your Intakes until you can close sales consistently.

Chapter 8 Summary

- How to avoid client discomfort when closing the sale
- Value Add-ons
- What to do, and not do, when clients are indecisive or hesitate
- How to answer, "Can I think about it?"
- Alternative sales

Chapter 9 - Setting Your Prices

Qualified Prices Attract Qualified Clients

You might think that clients will be dissuaded if you charge too much for your services. I thought that, too, in the early days. In time, what I've found is that high-quality clients are drawn to the higher priced, vetted services that you charge because most people assume they're going to get what they pay for. Quality clients know that an NBO who charges too low ($60 or less an hour) doesn't have confidence—clients know this! So it's important to set your feel-good prices because the higher they are within the range that feels good to you, the more you're going to attract high-quality clients who expect the high-quality services you already provide.

Let's talk about how you can set your price-points to reflect your growing, changing self-worth. Some of this section will be a review from what you've read earlier in the book, but I will add much more depth here due to its importance. It might be easier to grab a pen and paper for this, so you can reflect on how a price feels when you are looking at it.

Intuitive Pricing

Do the following exercise relaxed and alone (not in a client's presence):

Imagine the lowest number that you could charge for your services that still feels good to you. Decide what that dollar amount is per session. Let's say $75 per session feels good to you for a low price. Now, come up with the highest number that still feels good. Let's say $100 per session feels good. For both your low and high prices, notice when they start to feel uncomfortable, as in being too low and too high, respectively. Let's say you start feeling uncomfortable at $70 on the low end, and $110 on the high end. That's how you know when you're charging too little and too much per session. When you feel that uncomfortable threshold, back down a notch until both your low and high prices feel good. So I'll stay at $75 and $100, as an example.

Now, come up with the average of the low and high price. Add the two numbers and divide by two. 75+100=175/2=$88. How does $88 per session feel? It will probably feel good because it's within the range of what feels good to you. You could virtually choose use any number between $75 and $100 to refine which session price feels the best to you. Now you can annotate those numbers for your price sheet.

Another idea is that you could list $100 on your price sheet as your regular price, and $75 as your discounted price. That way, if you do choose to give a discount, it will never be below your lowest feel-good price of $75 per session. You won't compromise your self-worth either because you will have printed these prices on your price sheet. Reprint your price sheets to use with multiple clients.

I recommend not getting into the habit of using "sliding scale" pricing, but if you want to, stay within your lowest and highest feel-good prices that you've predetermined.

Congratulations! You've removed all of the ambiguity and the discomfort of talking about money with people when it comes to charging. You've decided what felt good to you to charge and what felt acceptable to you while not in the client's presence. You've eliminated qualifying your self-worth from the equation when talking to clients. You've tapped into what feels best to you on the low end and the high end. You're either using a sliding scale or an average number based on that range you defined. You're presenting it to the client when it's time to offer the sale and you've eliminated the temptation to low-ball your self-worth.

80% Rule Pricing

This pricing technique states that 80% of your clients should be buying, and 20% should not be buying. If 100% of the clients who walk through your door buy your services, this rule states you are not charging enough for your services; people may be seeing more value in your services than you see in yourself. On the other hand, if only 50% of clients are buying, your prices may be too high. Like Intuitive Pricing, you're still defining a range. Again, you don't want to charge too little and leave money on the table, and you don't want to turn clients away by charging too much. With the 80% Rule Pricing, your prices are correctly set if four out of every five clients are buying your services, on average.

Seasonal Pricing

Hotels raise their prices on the weekends. Flights are more expensive during the holidays. When business is slow, and there isn't enough demand to charge more, there may be enough incentive to charge less. When your business is in its busy season, you may have enough demand for your services to justify charging more. I've seen remote resort locations keep a certain price point on their rooms until the first reservation (or a certain number of reservations) is made after the slow season is nearing its end. These resorts allow the reservation frequency to determine when to raise their prices for the upcoming busy season.

What Ultimately Determines Session Prices

Your prices need to be high enough to make the money you need to stay in business and grow (profit higher than your expenses), but low enough so that most people can afford it. Many pricing strategies reduce to two major points: 1) the market average for your type of service (what NBO's in your industry charge for the same service within a certain range), and 2) the client's willingness to pay for your service. The better you get at your craft and the better results you can provide, the higher prices you can command.

Commanding Higher Prices

If you add more value for clients than other business owners do, you can command higher prices. When you're delivering more value, you're providing a better client experience and promoting better results. The more value you add, the more you can justify charging for it, especially if you're exceeding a client's expectations. Using value add-on offerings are a great way to achieve this. (Remember, value add-on offerings are items that do not require you to give more of your *time* to each client.)

Package Pricing Strategy

When listing prices on your website, you can offer a comparative "good, better, best" scenario. I used to offer a "regular" price, which was my baseline price. I didn't sell much at that level because clients always opted for the discounted packages. I offered a "better" option, which consisted of payment plans at a discounted rate of 25% off the regular price. Finally, I offered a "best" option which gave clients the maximum discount of 50% off their total package price if they paid in full. My "best" option was my lowest feel-good price point per session as discussed from the Intuitive Pricing section above.

Once you know your lowest feel-good price point, you can reverse engineer your package discounts. Using this pricing strategy, your lowest price point (and thus, your largest discount) will never be lower than what you feel good about earning. All of these packages should be written on your price sheet so that the client can visually assess and make distinctions among your package offerings and their respective discounts. You can even add the percentage discounts for each package to your price sheet if you like.

Hagglers

Clients who persistently bargain or dispute costs are commonly called "hagglers." For NBOs, hagglers are mostly coupon-holders attracted to novelty businesses look-ing for quick fixes and uninterested in taking responsibility for their change. These people try to manipulate you to lower your prices below your lowest feel-good price point. This is when you must say, "Sorry, I can't do that." But you can offer a value add-on offering (only if you want to work with them), and that usually suffices. If they try to negotiate further, it's haggling, and I recommend politely letting the client go. If this type of person pushes for a price reduction after you've presented your price sheet and discounted packages, it's a red flag. *Your price points are designed to qualify as well as disqualify clients.* You're not rejecting them; you are preserving your self-worth.

Everyone is lovable, even hagglers. But I emphasize their influence because boundaries are a weak spot for many NBOs due to people-pleasing and approval-seeking behaviors. Stand strong. Since you are in the business of offering deep transformation, you need to practice qualifying those who are ready and disqualifying those who aren't.

Chapter 9 Summary
- How to set your prices
- Discounts
- Alternative pricing
- Getting more money

Chapter 10 - Designing Packages

Why You Should Run Your Business Like a Chiropractor

Ⅰf you only go to a chiropractor on occasion when you need a spinal adjustment, your muscles will remain tense because they were out of alignment. But if you come back to the chiropractor regularly, your muscles will experience a continued improvement and hurt less after each alignment. Similarly, if you go to the gym once a month, you'll get some benefit; but if you go once per week, you'll get many more benefits. If you commit to doing long-term chiropractic care, you're going to get long-term results: less pain, more efficient organ function, more flexibility, less chance of injury, better sleep and digestion and more. Continual maintenance for self-care keeps you healthy and reduces setbacks.

Why should your business be any different than a chiropractor's? Are you in the business of symptom relief or long-term results and maintenance? Decide now. If you tell clients that it will take three months to give them the results they're wanting (within reason and without making guarantees), then design your packages for three months. You may find that certain emotional conditions generally take a range of time to transform, so plan for that in your business. If that's what it takes to give great results, then you'll attract clients who will pay for those results.

New NBOs tend to put all their self-worth on the line by trying to fix everything in one or two sessions and then *maybe* offering a package. Don't do that because it hurts your self-worth, makes you look needy, attracts victims, and doesn't create lasting change. You'll attract victims who will try to take advantage of the fact that you are attempting to do more than you can do in the time you allot. One or two sessions may be enough time for symptom relief, but generally, not enough time to create the lasting change they want.

You Set the Terms for How Long to Work with Clients

You are the authority in your business. You get to tell the client how long you need to work with them to produce optimal results. *Never try to produce results for the client in fewer sessions than you know you need to do your best work.* If you try to do four sessions worth of work in one session, you'll be rushed and sending the wrong messages to the client. Offer a range of sessions within multiple packages if necessary, and always give recommendations for what you think the client needs. (Again this is especially true for doing any emotionally transformative work for clients.) You must set the terms for how you *want* to work with clients, and these terms, most importantly, must feel good to you. If the terms feel good to you, then they will feel good to the client.

Designing Service Packages that Achieve Results

You will make more money and have happier clients by offering what you enjoy offering and what you're best at offering. Then, ask yourself how much time you need to achieve that result for them. Study how many sessions past clients have needed to get the results they've wanted, and continually re-design and sharpen your packages to improve. If you aren't currently doing this, take some time to ask yourself what kinds of long-term results you *could* offer to your clients. Then structure it out from there. And be sure to add homework. This way, you can move yourself along to higher self-worth.

At first, maybe you'll sell a 4-pack of sessions. Later maybe you'll offer a 6-pack or a 9-pack. Maybe you'll get even more confident and try to tackle deeper issues and offer a 12-pack of sessions to be completed once a week for three months. After some experimentation, you'll get a feel for what each client needs to transform their particular issues.

Offering packages of sessions keeps the client continually engaged. When a client commits to a package (vs. single sessions), they are experiencing an unraveling process in between the sessions. When you explain during the Intake process that the reason you want to work with them—for say, three months—is so you can help them achieve those deeper, lasting results, then you will be at ease when you ask for the sale. You will no longer worry about trying to please people in a short amount of time. You're giving yourself enough time to be peaceful about that result. You've managed their expectations about your recommended timeframes for working together.

Session frequency ultimately depends on you, but my standard was once per week. We could get clients their best results with one session per week or one session every two weeks at maximum. If you go longer than a couple of weeks, then the emotionally transformational work loses priority for the client. (Non-emotionally transformative services could go longer than two weeks.) Once per week works well for an emotionally transformative service.

Packages vs. Single Sessions

The reason you sell packages instead of single sessions is so you can continue greater in-depth processes and so the client can report back to you with their homework and transformational process in their lives while they are taking responsibility.

When a client sees you regularly for single sessions, they treat it like a novelty. When a client sees you regularly for a package, it's structured completely different. Single sessions are for symptom relief. Packages address root causes. Single sessions are for sticking a toe in the water. Packages are for making deep dives with a specific purpose. This is why I emphasize homework so much; it's for accountability.

If you are selling packages of sessions, and the client isn't *applying* what you're working on in between sessions, you've made a wrong turn. You likely: 1) didn't qualify the client properly, or 2) didn't express what the package is for and outline how it is to be used.

You are not selling packages to allow the client to redeem their sessions whenever they want. You are selling packages to create accountability and transformation in a deliberate timeframe.

Naming Your Service Packages

You can name your service packages to illustrate what your transformation might encompass. I used to call my packages: 6-pack, 9-pack or 12-pack. Or, you can give your packages names to illustrate the benefits of your proposed solutions, such as: "Empowerment Package," "Overhaul Package," or "Face-Lift Package." Names make it easier for clients to choose versus having them stare at packages that only feature numbers of sessions. The more specific you are, the easier it will be for a client to connect with your solution.

Contracts

For pay-in-full contracts and payment plan contracts, list your packages and single session prices with the client's name and debit card information and store in a secure place or use an electronic auto-debit system to avoid storing debit card information on paper. I would include a standard 3-day money back guarantee or refund policy if the client wants to back out. After three days from signing, they're locked into the contract. Go over this verbally with the client to ensure they understand. Less than 10 percent will choose to back out of a contract, and it is fair to offer a back out option. If you're not sure, ask yourself, "What would I want a contract to include before I invest a substantial amount of money on myself?"

Chapter 10 Summary

- Gyms and Chiropractors
- Rushing results
- Packages vs. single sessions
- Contracts and refunds

Conclusion

We've covered a lot in this book: self-worth, selling, systems and more. I've provided education not only on how to sell to clients, but I've also guided you on how you can structure your business so that you can protect your self-worth as well as continually improve how you run your business. In time, you may even teach other people how to work in your business!

You now have tools, techniques, systems—and most importantly—education on how you need to think about your business.

Businesses aren't just about having a skill or talent, a space to see clients and a bank account. Businesses are living, breathing things that require our care and attention. Selling is just one part of a business, although, a very important part. With what you've learned here, you'll find that making sales is enjoyable, easy, rewarding and abundant!

By implementing what I've taught in this book, you will help both your clients and your business to grow. As you maximize your strengths and create systems to protect your self-worth and produce predictable results, you can go further than you've imagined possible.

I have achieved proven success by using these strategies. If I can start from scratch with no business background, and in a few years, get to where I am—using these strategies will make you successful too!

You know that building a business takes work—lots of work. But it doesn't need to be a struggle. I invite you to make the changes that you know you can make to be successful. You have templates. You have tools. You have my support. Now go out there and make it happen. I believe in you.

About the Author

Todd Schaefer is a holistic business coach and consultant who helps business owners to create customized, effective business practices based on spiritual principles that mirror their values and vision. Todd helps them resolve self-worth, organizational and operational challenges to become legitimate, profitable businesses.

As hypnotherapists and life coaches, Todd and his wife created a multi-six-figure business from nothing and helped over 4,000 clients address their personal challenges, empowering them to improve their lives. In 2014, Todd was voted "Life Coach of the Year" by *Mental Health Magazine,* and his business was voted "Mental Health Provider of the Year."

For more of Todd's work, see *The Acceptance Guidebook: Spiritual Solutions for Active Minds*, which is based on *A Course in Miracles.*

For Todd's coaching, consulting and speaking engagements, contact kyra@asyouwishpublishing.com.

www.ingramcontent.com/pod-product-compliance
Lightning Source LLC
Chambersburg PA
CBHW071715210326
41597CB00017B/2486